THE LAST MILLENNIUM

THE LAST MILLENNIUM

A REVEALING LOOK AT THE REMARKABLE DAYS AHEAD AND HOW YOU CAN LIVE THEM TO THE FULLEST

MAC HAMMOND

Harrison House
Tulsa, OK

The Last Millennium—
A Revealing Look at the Remarkable Days Ahead
and How You Can Live Them to the Fullest
ISBN 1-57794-239-6
Copyright © 1999 by Mac Hammond
P.O. Box 29469
Minneapolis, MN 55429

Published by Harrison House, Inc.
P.O. Box 35035
Tulsa, Oklahoma 74153

CONTENTS

INTRODUCTION

The year is A.D. 96. The Roman emperor Domitian has decreed that Christianity must be eradicated. The apostle John is now the last surviving disciple who actually walked with Jesus. And across the vast Roman Empire, fragile, fledgling churches are looking to him for leadership.

Of course, the Roman government knows this too and is determined to kill John. However, nothing they do manages to succeed—not even boiling him in oil!

That shouldn't come as a surprise. You see, by this time John is widely known as the "Apostle of Love." He is the one who has the greatest revelation of the Lord's love for us. He even calls himself "the disciple whom Jesus loved." (John 13:23; 20:2; 21:7,20.)

In reality, John's revelation of God's amazing love for His own causes him to function in the power of that love to such a degree they *cannot* kill him. Why? Because love never fails. (1 Cor. 13:8.)

When the Roman government realizes they cannot kill the Apostle of Love, they do the next best thing. They minimize his influence by exiling him to a tiny, barren island called Patmos in the Aegean Sea, fifty miles southwest of Ephesus. Not a single tree stands on the four-mile-wide, nine-mile-long upthrust of blistering rock and sand. They put him there to die as so many thousands of others have before him!

Instead, he receives a supernatural visitation from heaven and writes the book of Revelation.

Initially, it was written in letter form and addressed to seven young churches in Asia Minor—churches John had visited, nurtured and instructed.

As with letters we write today, it had an introduction and a conclusion.

Chapter 1 of Revelation is the introduction. Chapters 2 and 3 are the instructions to the seven different churches—each church receiving a letter with its own specific set of instructions.

Chapters 4 through 21 are the text of the prophecy John was told he must relay to all seven churches. The closing of the letter begins in Revelation 22:8 and goes till the end of the book.

As you approach this extraordinary book, the first thing to keep in mind is that John did not author Revelation; he wrote it down, but he was not the source of it. He makes this clear right from the very beginning when he writes:

John, to the seven churches which are in Asia: Grace to you and peace from Him who is and who was and who is to come, and from the seven Spirits who are before His throne.

Revelation 1:4

It is obvious the phrase *from Him who is and who was and who is to come,* refers to God the Father—the Eternal One. The seven spirits which are before His throne refer to the sevenfold anointing of the Holy Spirit. (Isa. 11:2.)

Contrary to what some liberal scholars have suggested, John was not suffering from sunstroke when he wrote Revelation. What we read in Revelation is an accurate representation of what John truly was shown.

God considers the book of Revelation to be so important that He assigned both blessings and curses to it—blessings for reading, hearing and doing and curses for adding, subtracting or changing. (Rev. 22:18,19.)

Yes, we should approach this book with a great deal of reverence and respect. But we should also approach it with excitement and expectancy.

You see, Revelation is God's "game plan" for the end times. And if we want to win, we must understand what that game plan is.

What This Book Is *Not*

One final note before we dive into the text of this amazing book called Revelation. What you now hold in your hands is not another Bible prophecy book. My purpose in writing is not to offer another in-depth examination of end-time events. There is already a large body of fine work available on this subject. I see no need to add to it.

What I don't see when I scan the bookshelves of my local Christian bookstore are books that help the believer apply the wonderful truths and prophecies of Revelation to his daily life—books that help you walk through these extraordinary days in peace and victory.

That is what I hope you'll take away from this book. My prayer is that as these end-time events unfold in the days ahead, you'll be ready and able to live them for all they're worth.

CHAPTER ONE

The Last Millennium

We are the generation that will not only see the end of one millennium and the beginning of the next, but we are also the generation that will usher in the last millennium. What a privileged group we are!

I can just imagine Abraham, Moses, all of the apostles and Paul looking down from heaven and saying, "Oh, I wish I could be in their shoes!"

The focus of our study is the last millennium—specifically, the transition from our present millennium to the next and final one. Then we'll examine the composition of that final thousand years. This is what the book of Revelation is about.

A Clearly Defined Reason

It is important that we have a clearly defined reason for studying the book of Revelation. Doing so helps us know what we are exercising our faith for.

Too often the approach to end times is motivated by casual interest or a sensationalistic curiosity. Not this time. God has directed me to write on this subject because our understanding of end times is the strongest motivator there is to right living.

In our generation, most people simply scoff when it comes to things like the Rapture of the church or the literal establishment of the reign of Jesus upon this earth. Those things are unreal to them, so they stay in the comfortable realm of fantasy and mock whatever threatens that fantasy.

The New Testament anticipated such skeptics:

> **Knowing this first: that scoffers will come in the last days, walking according to their own lusts, and saying, "Where is the promise of His coming? For since the fathers fell asleep, all things continue as they were from the beginning of creation.**
>
> **2 Peter 3:3**

If you make light of the end times—if it is not real to you—the probability is that you will indeed fulfill the lusts of your flesh. You will not reflect nor participate in God's will for you or the majority of His blessings.

God's Greatest Harvest

Many Christians wonder why so much time has passed since John penned the words of Revelation and the complete fulfillment of the prophecies he recorded.

The fact is, God is waiting until the greatest possible harvest of souls can be received into the kingdom.

> **The Lord is not slack concerning His promise, as some count slackness, but is longsuffering toward us, not willing that any should perish but that all should come to repentance.**
>
> **2 Peter 3:9**

> **Therefore be patient, brethren, until the coming of the Lord. See how the farmer waits for the precious fruit of the**

**earth, waiting patiently for it until it receives the early and
latter rain. You also be patient. Establish your hearts, for
the coming of the Lord is at hand.**

James 5:7,8

Even though God is omniscient and knows precisely when the day of complete fulfillment is, it has not been set. The fullness of time is dependent on the gospel being preached to all of the world—"the precious fruit of the earth" being ready.

**But the day of the Lord will come as a thief in the night,
in the which the heavens will pass away with a great noise,
and the elements will melt with fervent heat; both the earth
and the works that are in it will be burned up.**

2 Peter 3:10

You can know the times and the seasons, but you cannot know the day. The Day of the Lord signals the 1000-year period of time when Jesus is in literal residence on this earth as King of kings and Lord of lords; it signals the millennial reign of Christ—the last millennium.

Digging a Little Deeper

The Bible has a startling warning for the people of this generation: The things the world says are important are going to be dissolved in a blink, consumed by the fire of God.

**Therefore, since all these things will be dissolved, what
manner of persons ought you to be in holy conduct and
godliness, looking for and hastening the coming of the day
of God, because of which the heavens will be dissolved
being on fire, and the elements will melt with fervent heat?**

2 Peter 3:11,12

Considering that, shouldn't we be living a life separated unto God? living for God? walking with God?

Now, it is not coincidence that the Holy Spirit said **the day of the Lord** in verse 10 and **the day of God** in verse 12. Jesus is the King of kings and Lord of lords; His "day" represents the 1000 years of His reign upon this earth. God is eternal, and with Him there is no time. So the **day of God** is speaking of the beginning of the eternal state.

We find a remarkable truth in this passage. We are encouraged to be **looking for and hastening the coming of the day of God.** In other words, our attitudes and lives have an effect on the return of the Lord!

The hungrier you are for this present age to end and for the millennial reign of Jesus to begin, the quicker these things will come to pass. I think you will see the connection between these two things as we continue our study. You see, it is one of the elements having to do with the "fullness of time" which must arrive before the end times begin.

The Greek word translated *looking* in this passage literally means an earnest anticipation and expectation.[1] God wants you to have a great anticipation of the eternal state—the day of God. He wants you to be mindful of and motivated by an understanding of your eternal destiny.

The Word says this life here is but a blink of an eye in time—nothing but a vapor. There is an eternity beyond the veil of death awaiting each one of us. The difficulty is that we do not have enough of an understanding of our true eternal destiny to be eagerly anticipating and looking for that day.

The truth is, you will be ruling and reigning with Jesus for an eternity—and not over just a few square feet of terra firma either but over the vastness of a universe yet to be explored. And we get to explore it!

We get to explore galaxies by the billions, each galaxy containing millions of suns and planetary bodies. Who knows how many other kinds of life are present in this universe?

People ask me all the time, "Do you believe in extraterrestrial life?"

They're often surprised when I answer, "Of course I do; the Bible teaches it." It mentions winged creatures and four-headed beasts, not to mention the angelic hosts. They are out there, and God says He needs us to rule and reign with Him over the vastness of this creation for eons to come. It is going to put science fiction movies to shame.

I am not saying this just to be sensational. This is what the Word of God says. We just need to let our minds and expectations move beyond the parameters of religious tradition. You have an eternal destiny awaiting you that is so magnificent in its scope that it is impossible to embrace right now. But we get glimpses of it in the Word.

This destiny is going to be determined by the way we live our lives now. This life is but a blink of an eye, yet it determines our experience of eternity. Read on to find out how.

Raised to Rulership

In Matthew 25, Jesus relates a parable in which a lord returns from his journey to a far country. He had entrusted all of his belongings to three of his servants, and two of them have brought increase to the lord's estate. He says to each, **Well done, good and faithful servant; you have been faithful over a few things, I will make you ruler over many things** (v. 23).

The wonderful reality is that you are called to rule and reign with Jesus. But the amount of responsibility you are given on an eternal scale depends upon your stewardship of the resources God entrusts to you in *this* life. It does not matter how much he entrusts to you; it only matters what you do with what you receive.

In the parable, one servant was given five talents, one was given two talents and the third was given one talent. To the ones who increased their talents, the lord gave the same commendation. So it is not a matter of amount but what you do with it that's important.

What are you doing with the time and resources you have? What are you doing to bring increase to the kingdom of God? It's not a matter of finding the highest yielding mutual fund for your money; the way you bring increase to God's kingdom is through the principle of sowing and reaping.

The Purpose of Revelation

The purpose of the book of Revelation is to make us aware of our need to be mindful of eternity awaiting us and to live our lives accordingly.

This life, which seems so demanding and consumes our attention, is nothing, friend. We have to become eternally minded. We have to focus on the unseen realm revealed by the Word, not the temporal realm we live in, which is subject to change.

Nevertheless we, according to His promise, look for new heavens and a new earth in which righteousness dwells. Therefore, beloved, looking forward to these things, be diligent to be found by Him in peace, without spot and blameless.

2 Peter 3:13,14

As we look for the Day of the Lord, we begin to move toward the place of holiness and separation, where we become the glorious church without spot or wrinkle. (Eph. 5:27.)

There is no other spiritual principle in the Word which has this kind of effect on a person's behavior.

One More Night With the Frogs

Unless there is a sense of urgency in our lives, we have a tendency to say, "Tomorrow, Lord. I'll do that tomorrow."

The truth of the matter is this: Our flesh, our unregenerate nature, always wants to put God and His direction for our lives off till another time. We see this from the beginning of the Bible to the end.

We see an example of this in chapter 8 of Exodus during one of the ten plagues which came on Egypt—frogs!

The curses which came against Egypt came because of their decision to resist the direction of God, and He responded by removing His hand of protection, allowing the curse to manifest in different ways. One of those ways was a plague of frogs.

Can you imagine what it was like? Frogs in the fridge, the oven, the bed, your underwear, the bathroom. Frogs everywhere. Big frogs. Little frogs. Slimy frogs. Horny toad frogs.

The Bible says:

Then Pharaoh called for Moses and Aaron, and said, "Entreat the Lord that He may take away the frogs from me and from my people; and I will let the people go, that they may sacrifice to the Lord."

Exodus 8:8

But when Moses asked him, "When do you want me to ask the Lord?" Pharaoh said, "Tomorrow."

Can you imagine? Pharaoh wanted one more night with the frogs!

Amazing, isn't it? Yet, this is the tendency of our unregenerate nature as well—to resist the direction of God, even though it perpetuates the curse in our lives.

You see, the frogs represent the curse in the earth. Even though our deliverance from sickness, poverty and oppression is in God, we tend to say, "Tomorrow, Lord. Just give me one more night with the frogs."

I wonder how many people have gone to hell saying, "Tomorrow, Lord." But it is not just unbelievers who say this. Christians say it all the time when confronted by His direction in their lives.

"I'll bring my tithe to the storehouse tomorrow."

"I'll start praying a little more tomorrow."

"I'll love my wife sacrificially tomorrow."

"I'll be submitted to my husband tomorrow."

"I'll get involved in a ministry tomorrow."

No, you won't. When tomorrow comes, you will say the same old things again. Time and again—whether it's to the written Word or the Spirit of God to our hearts, we say "Tomorrow, Lord" and then wonder why there are still frogs in our underwear.

Sometimes we get mad at God: "God, what are these frogs doing in my life?" They're there because you put off God's direction and perpetuated the curse in your life.

A Revival of Urgency

What is the solution for this tendency? We have to develop a greater sense of urgency about being doers of the Word of God, about bringing our lives more in line with the Word and about experiencing a deeper intimacy with God.

Revival is really not a group event. It often happens in groups, but revival is supposed to occur in an individual's heart first. If you have to continually go to revival meetings for their fire to "light your wood" and keep it burning, you are missing the point.

Starting and sustaining the fire of personal revival in your heart requires a desire and a hunger for God rather than an appetite for the world.

It also requires a strong conviction of your need to change. If you are not convicted of your need to change, you will not have your hunger for God filled. You can be hungry for God—you can even know you really need to change—but without a sense of urgency, you will still say, "Tomorrow, Lord" and continue to sleep with the frogs.

Developing Urgency

According to the Word, there are three ways urgency is born in the human heart.

First, you must get fed up with the frogs. There will come a day when you have had it with the frogs. You have to come to the place where you have absolutely no tolerance any longer for the curse of sin and death encroaching on your life.

Too often we allow the curse to touch us without taking a stand against it. We need to become like David when the Philistines oppressed Israel and Goliath had them completely intimidated. David said, "Enough is enough. Who is going to take up this cause? No one? Then I will do it!" (1 Sam. 17:26,32.)

When are you going to get fed up with the curse in your life? When are you going to get sick and tired of the enemy's encroaching on your territory when he has no right to? When are you going to become righteously indignant at the continuing sickness, poverty, lack or oppression in your life? Getting sick of them is one of the ways urgency is born in your heart.

The more you realize the enemy has no *right* to be in any area of your life, the more real it becomes to you that you do not *have* to be sick, poor or oppressed. God redeemed you from the curse of the law. The more real that becomes to you, the closer you come to saying, "Enough is enough!" and acting in faith.

Urgency Today

The second thing which contributes to a healthy sense of urgency in the human heart is the realization that you may not have a tomorrow. I do not mean this in a melodramatic sense.

God said that we choose between life and death, blessing or cursing. But the only way we know about the choices we can make is through the revelation of the Holy Spirit and His ministry in our lives.

When you resist the Holy Spirit's leading, you do something the Bible calls hardening your heart. The first time the Holy Spirit directs you in a particular way, especially as it regards living a separated life and living right before God, it is painful.

But if you do *not* respond to Him, you begin to harden in that area. Every time you say, "No, I'm not going to do that," your heart gets a little harder and it gets a little easier to say no. The next time it is harder to hear the Holy Spirit. If you continue to refuse Him, you will stop hearing His voice altogether and the Spirit will be quenched in you.

So the point is this: Every time you hear from the Holy Spirit, respond!

You may not have a tomorrow, and you may not have another opportunity to make the change you need to make. You cannot make the changes in just your own strength; you will need the Holy Spirit to help you.

The Urgent Future

The third thing which will put urgency in your heart is looking for the day of God. This involves not only the return of the Lord, but knowing that the days beyond are going to bring the unfolding of God's plan—through the last millennium and on into eternity.

Earnestly anticipating and expecting those things as a part of life's present experience will motivate you to elevate your quality of life and enable you to become the glorious church.

This kind of reality must be born in your heart. That is why it is vital to study the last millennium.

An Overview of the Events To Come

Before we dive in to the text of Revelation, let me give you a brief summary of the chronological events the Word gives us to mark the end of this millennium, the transition to the last millennium and on into the eternal state.

The Rapture of the Church

The age we live in is typically called the church age or the dispensation of the Holy Spirit. According to the Word, it ends with something commonly called the Rapture, or the catching away of the church. Jesus will appear in the clouds, and the dead in Christ will rise first. Then we who are the believing church will rise to meet Him in the air. (1 Thess. 4:16,17.)

Daniel's Seventieth Week – The Tribulation

After the Rapture, a seven-year period of time often referred to as "Daniel's Seventieth Week" begins. This is the uncompleted last seven years of the Jewish dispensation in which the Lord will finish his dealings with Israel.

That seven-year period of time is also called the Tribulation, and it represents the greatest outpouring of God's judgment and wrath upon this world the earth has ever seen. The Tribulation will end with the Second Advent, or the coming of Jesus Christ.

Armageddon

The principle events in this season of time will be the battle of Armageddon, the defeat of the Antichrist and the establishment of Jesus' earthly reign. This marks the beginning of the last millennium.

Satan Cast Into the Abyss

The Word shows us that at the beginning of the last millennium, Satan is going to be cast into the bottomless pit and chained there for the majority of this period **so that he should deceive the nations no more till the thousand years were finished** (Rev. 20:3).

A Thousand Years of Peace With Jesus as Ruler

We will experience life in the last millennium free of the deception which has harassed mankind ever since the Garden of Eden. Mankind is going to experience life on this planet under a divinely appointed system of government.

For 1000 years God is going to give mankind every opportunity possible to exercise his freedom of choice without the distracting influence of Satan and deception in order to allow man to align his life and his purpose with God's purpose.

Satan Released After 1000 Years

Then at the end of that 1000 years, Satan will be released from the bottomless pit for a short while to deceive whom he may. As astounding as it may sound, he will deceive multitudes in that short time frame—even people who have lived on this earth with Jesus for 1000 years without deception but with freedom from all the schemes of the devil and the world's curse.

The point of all this is to bring the earth to a place where as many human beings as possible can be secured for God's eternal purpose. Then the end of the world as we know it will come.

The Great White Throne Judgment

At the end of the millennial reign, we have what is called the Great White Throne Judgment. Everyone alive and all of the dead—who will be raised to life again—will have to stand before this judgment seat.

All of those who have aligned their lives with Satan and his demonic host will be cast into the lake of fire to dwell there in utter torment for all eternity.

Purification by Fire and a New Heaven and Earth

The earth at that time will be so corrupted by the sin and deception which has been in it since Satan's release from the bottomless pit that it will be destroyed and purified by the fire of God.

Then a completely new heaven and new earth will be formed, at the end of which God will transplant the New Jerusalem, the capital city of heaven right now, onto the planet earth. He will then forever take up residence with His creation (mankind) here on earth.

This marks the end of the last millennium and the beginning of the eternal state.

Now we will take a look at how the book of Revelation itself is structured.

CHAPTER TWO

The Book of Revelation: An Overview

Do not look at the book of Revelation as though it were penned by a old man on a desert island who had eaten some bad pizza.

Revelation is not supposed to be the book of confusion. It is a book which reveals. We are supposed to understand it and what it tells us about end times.

By contrast, when God gave Daniel prophecies about the end times, He said, **"...for the words are closed up and sealed till the time of the end"** (Dan. 12:9).

But at the end of the book of Revelation, the angel who appears to the apostle John said, **"Do not seal the words of the prophecy of this book, for the time is at hand"** (Rev. 22:10).

We can understand Revelation if we approach it according to the Lord's direction to John in Revelation 1:19. The Lord said to John, **"Write**

the things which you have seen, and the things which are, and the things which will take place after this."

This is a major key to understanding the book. There are three divisions in the book of Revelation:

1. The things which you have seen—past tense.
2. The things which are—present tense.
3. The things which will take place after this—future tense.

"The things which you have seen" refers to the past, from John's perspective and time frame.

"The things which are" refers to the time from when John was writing, through the present day up till the end of the church age and the beginning of the last millennium.

It also refers to the letters to the seven churches. Those seven churches were a representation of the challenges all churches were going to face.

"The things which will take place after this" starts at the beginning of chapter 4 where John says he was "caught up into heaven." What we see here is a type of the Rapture of the church. So from chapter 4 on, he is talking about the time after the Rapture of the church.

One of the common mistakes people make in end-time theology is finding something in Revelation 17 or 18 and saying, "Aha! I see that happening right now; it was on the news just the other night." No. Something in those chapters falls into the category of "after this," after the church is gone. What you saw was a shadow of something far more extreme which is to come.

Things Which Must Shortly Take Place

The revelation of Jesus Christ, which God gave Him to show His servants—things which must shortly take place. And He sent and signified it by His angel to His servant John, who bore witness to the word of God, and to the testimony of Jesus Christ, to all things that he saw.

Revelation 1:1,2

In these verses, we learn that the book of Revelation was given to show things, or events, that must shortly take place. John's vision of Jesus underscores the word *shortly*.

Our understanding of the book of Revelation needs to be grounded in a basic dividing of those events into certain categories and an establishment of their chronological order.

Overview

Following the introduction of verses 1 through 8, *the first section* is the revelation John receives of Jesus Himself through the vision he has. It is an open vision, not a dream; he did not close his eyes and daydream. He turned around, and there stood the glorified Christ. Jesus revealed Himself to authenticate the revelations and prophecy to come. John reacts, and then Jesus' instructions to him begin.

The second section is Revelation 2 and 3, which have to do with the events which must shortly come to pass in the next 2000-year time period, the church age. We should not view the seven letters to the churches in Asia as instruction just to the churches of that day or to those churches in particular. Although their situations are what prompted the letters, we know the Word of God is for eternal instruction, applicable to any age no matter who did the writing.

Even though the apostle Paul wrote his letters to specific churches, the principles he promoted, discussed and summarized are for all of the church in all ages. The Word is timeless. Just as God is timeless, so is His Word. He and His Word are one.

All of the churches existing worldwide during the 2000-year period of time called the church age are going to experience some, or all, of the things we read about regarding the churches in the book of Revelation.

The Lord is saying, "These are the ways the enemy will come against you, common mistakes you will make, what you will need to do to correct those mistakes and things you will need to be aware of."

Even more significantly, these letters apply to us as individuals. Not only is there a universal church and a local church; there is also the individual church. You are called a **temple of the Holy Spirit** (1 Cor. 6:19). You have become the church. If there were only one Christian left in the world, the church would still be here.

For example, to the first church the Lord addresses, the church at Ephesus, He says, "You have done a lot of good works, but I have one problem with you: You have left your first love." Not only is that applicable to many churches today, but it is also the sad condition of many individual believers.

It is easy for us get excited about what God is doing. We establish outreaches and plan programs and get so busy meeting needs that we forget about our first love. Who is that? It is Jesus, the One who brought us into the kingdom of God in the first place. Maintaining a close relationship with Him is vital to our continuing growth and experience of God.

The third section of events which must shortly take place is in Revelation 4 and 5: the events which occur in heaven immediately after the Rapture of the church.

There is a clear discernment of the Rapture of the church as we study the book of Revelation. We can see it very easily. If you have been wondering whether the church is going to be here during the Tribulation and whether or not you need to go buy guns, ammunition and food and head for the mountains, the answer is no.

God said the church is not appointed unto wrath. He is going to catch away the saints who are alive as well as raise those who have gone before them in death.

The Rapture will occur right at the close of the church age. At the end of the letters to the churches, opening chapter 4, we see the events that are going to occur in heaven immediately after the Rapture, during a time frame coinciding with the seven years of Tribulation here on earth.

The fourth section of events is found in Revelation 6-19. This section is a revelation of what will be happening on earth during the Tribulation, Daniel's Seventieth Week, the final seven years of the Jewish Dispensation. Whatever you want to call it; they are all one and the same. There are scattered occasional references to heaven, but only so we can have a better understanding of what is happening here on earth.

The fifth section is Revelation 20, which describes the last millennium. It tells of the establishment of the physical, literal, earthly reign of Jesus, the binding of Satan and his banishment to the bottomless pit, our 1000 years of reigning together with Christ, the release of Satan at the end of that time, his subsequent deception of the nations and finally Satan's defeat and final banishment into the lake of fire.

The sixth section of events is from Revelation 21-22:8. This is a description of the transition from the last millennium to the eternal state and then a look at what our lives will be like for the rest of eternity.

Finally, *the seventh section* is from Revelation 22:8 to the end of the book. This is John's conclusion to his letters and the book of Revelation.

The Blessings of Prophecy

Blessed is he who reads and those who hear the words of this prophecy, and keep those things which are written in it; for the time is near.

Revelation 1:3

If you study the Greek, the word *blessed* means "to empower to prosper";[1] it is a direct reference to God's enabling you to increase in accordance with His promises. This means God has made available the anointing to experience the increase of His promises of peace, joy, good health and prosperity.

This verse also implies an increased level of blessing in three ways. There is an increase which comes if you not only read the prophecy, but if you hear the words of this prophecy as well.

But this is not just talking about hearing with a natural ear. The Word says on several occasions, **"He who has an ear, let him hear what the Spirit says."** The word *hearing* in Revelation 1:3 refers to your ability to hear what the Spirit of God is saying through these verses. The Word says, **Faith comes by hearing, and hearing by the word of God** (Rom. 10:17). You do not get faith by hearing a Scripture one time.

In the same sense, you are not going to get blessed by hearing the words of this prophecy one time. "Hearing" is in the continuous sense. In other words, God wants you to hear it enough that faith comes and you know you live in "that day"; it becomes reality to you. Then you will experience the increased measure of blessing.

The highest level of blessing comes to those who **keep those things which are written in it.** Once you have heard this word and it has become reality to you, it produces that urgency in you to be a doer of the Word, to take care of things and to keep this prophecy alive and active in your life.

How do you keep a prophecy—something that, by its very nature, has not yet come to pass? You base your life on what you have heard; begin acting in faith on what you have heard, knowing the time is at hand for these things to occur. You start doing the things the prophecy instructs you to do in preparation for its fulfillment.

Revelation and Time

The powerful imagery of the book of Revelation can sometimes tend to obscure the simple structure of the book. If you remember that Revelation deals with the three time periods we have seen in this chapter—past, present and future—it will be much easier to understand the imagery and its role in the fulfillment of all things.

Remember, our job is to read, hear and do what the prophecy instructs us to do. Keep that in mind as we continue in our study.

CHAPTER THREE

Operating in the Spirit

It is so important to see this life for what it really is in order to prepare for the eternity which is to come. Our jobs, spouses, kids, health and friends, while being important, are not the sum total of this life. This temporary state is only training for our lives in the eternal state.

Revelation 1:5-6 gives us critical insight into the two most important elements for understanding the framework in which we are to live.

> **And from Jesus Christ, the faithful witness, the first-born from the dead, and the ruler over the kings of the earth. To Him who loved us and washed us from our sins in His own blood, and has made us kings and priests to His God and Father, to Him be glory and dominion forever and ever. Amen.**

The first insight is found in the phrase **firstborn from the dead.** Jesus is "the firstborn from the dead." Well, if there is a firstborn there has to be a secondborn, thirdborn and so forth. If you have accepted Jesus as your Lord and Savior, your number is in there somewhere. You have experienced a new birth in your spirit. When you were born again, your spirit was made alive. But upon Jesus' return, bodily resurrection is going to follow as well.

The second insight is found in the phrase **has made us kings and priests.** This is past tense; it is already a done deal if you are born again. The Lord has called us to be kings and priests. What does a king do? He reigns with absolute authority, and every resource in his kingdom is at his disposal to promote his purpose. This is what we are going to be doing eternally. Kings are appointed for life; and since we will never die spiritually, we will never cease to rule and reign with Christ.

But God wants us to begin now. He has made us kings and priests *right now;* that is part of the preparation for our eternal destiny.

Let that sink down into your heart. That is what we are called to do and to be, more than anything else. That calling transcends any denomination, faction, branch, ministry or organization. The most basic calling we have in common is to rule and reign with Jesus for an eternity. Our destiny is to rule with Him.

Now, in that process we are not the "top dog." We serve Him, but we serve Him by reigning over the vastness of creation on His behalf for eons to come. Another term the Bible uses for this is "being His stewards." What a steward does is exercise the full authority and power of his lord to manage his household and estate for him.

That means we exercise God's dominion and authority to manage His affairs on His behalf. He has given us His name, dominion, power and authority, and we are to use them as He wills in this earth, as well as in the eternal state.

What we do in this life as God's stewards will determine the extent of our destiny, the shape our role takes for eternity. If this ever hits home with you, it will make you think more than once about the decisions you make each day.

The Parable of the Talents

The parable of the talents in Matthew 25 is an example of this truth. The master goes on a journey to a far country and entrusts his belongings to his three servants. This is a type of Jesus' ascension into heaven to be seated at the right hand of the Father, while we oversee the work here on earth until His return.

Two of the servants invested their portions and brought increase to the master, while the third hid his portion in the ground. When the master returned, the servants had to give an account for what they had done while he'd been gone.

The master said to the two who had brought increase to his kingdom, **"Well done, good and faithful servant; you were faithful over a few things, I will make you ruler over many things. Enter into the joy of your lord"** (Matt. 25:21).

The extent of your eternal rulership depends on how faithful you are to use the resources He has entrusted to you to bring an increase to His kingdom in this earth. You cannot read that parable any other way.

How faithful have we been to produce increase in the kingdom of God?

Priests Unto Our God

We are priests as well as kings. That means, unlike people in the Old Testament, we no longer have to go through a person to get to God. *We* are the temple of the Holy Spirit; He lives in us. We have immediate access to the Trinity anytime we want. We can be closer to Him than we are to our spouses.

We are a royal priesthood and kings with absolute dominion over our circumstances.

There is not one single circumstance confronting you to which you must bow your knee.

The devil has squeezed these two truths out of God's Word by the tradition of man. That is why Jesus told the religious leaders of His day that they were **"making the word of God of no effect through your tradition"** (Mark 7:13).

Every Eye Will See Him

Behold, He is coming with clouds, and every eye will see Him, even they who pierced Him. And all the tribes of the earth will mourn because of Him. Even so, Amen.

Revelation 1:7

This verse has been a source of some confusion, so let me help clarify it for you. The question is whether this verse refers to the Rapture of the church or the second coming of Jesus. At the Rapture of the church no one sees Him but the church. Here, His enemies see Him, so this has to be the second coming.

Later chapters of Revelation also indicate that not every one is going to know Jesus has returned to earth. That is why there will be missionaries during the Millennium. There are going to be nations of people who do not know Jesus is even here, and the Jewish nation is going to provide His primary emissaries in spreading the Word of His grace.

While many will see the second coming of the Lord and not know what it is or that Jesus is now on the earth, everyone will know something remarkable has happened.

They who pierced Him is not a reference to the literal people who crucified Him, but to those who continue to pierce Him with their mockery and resistance to Him.

All the tribes of earth will mourn because of Him—except the church. We will be gone already. That is the whole point: The people who are left will be the enemies of the Cross. Christ will return in all His glory, and people will see what they have rejected. I would mourn, too, if I were in their shoes.

John's Revelation of Christ

"I am the Alpha and the Omega, the Beginning and the End," says the Lord, who is and who was and who is to come, the Almighty" (Rev. 1:8). After this verse announces who the Revelator of the vision is, John introduces himself and in verse 10 begins to tell his vision.

I was in the Spirit on the Lord's Day, and I heard behind me a loud voice, as of a trumpet, saying, "I am the Alpha and the Omega, the First and the Last," and, "What you see, write in a book and send it to the seven churches which are

in Asia: to Ephesus, to Smyrna, to Pergamos, to Thyatira, to Sardis, to Philadelphia, and to Laodicea."

Then I turned to see the voice that spoke with me. And having turned, I saw seven golden lampstands, and in the midst of the seven lampstands One like the Son of Man, clothed with a garment down to the feet and girded about the chest with a golden band. His head and hair were white like wool, as white as snow, and His eyes like a flame of fire; His feet were like fine brass, as if refined in a furnace, and His voice as the sound of many waters; He had in His right hand seven stars, out of His mouth went a sharp two-edged sword, and His countenance was like the sun shining in its strength.

And when I saw Him, I fell at His feet as dead. But He laid His right hand on me, saying to me, "Do not be afraid; I am the First and the Last. I am He who lives, and was dead, and behold, I am alive forevermore. Amen. And I have the keys of Hades and of Death.

"Write the things which you have seen, and the things which are, and the things which will take place after this. The mystery of the seven stars which you saw in My right hand, and the seven golden lampstands: The seven stars are the angels of the seven churches, and the seven lampstands which you saw are the seven churches."

Revelation 1:10-20

What John describes here is a vision not of a baby in a manger or of a man on a cross or in a tomb; but this is the glorified Christ appearing in all of His majesty and glory. What an overwhelming moment this must have been!

Understanding the Symbols

What are the stars? What are the candlesticks? What is the sword? The best way to understand this is to let the Scripture speak for itself.

Jesus identifies the seven stars as the angels of the seven churches; and the seven candlesticks surrounding Him are the seven churches themselves.

Of course, if it is going to be the church of the Lord Jesus Christ, He must be in the middle; He must be the focal point. However, He is not going to direct His instructions regarding changes among men to the heavenly, supernatural beings called angels. So the **angels of the seven churches** obviously are not literal angels.

You may ask, "Well, what are they then?"

If you look up the word *angel* in the Greek, it simply means "messenger."[1] An angel can be any being God uses as a messenger. In the book of Revelation alone, the word is used twenty-seven times, and twenty-two of those times, it refers to a *human man.*

So who is God's messenger to the local church? The pastor. These are the ones to whom God has entrusted the message of salvation, healing, restoration and deliverance for the local congregation. The angels here are a reference to the pastors of the seven churches.

Being in the Spirit

I want you to see something important in verse 10: John said, **I was in the Spirit on the Lord's Day, and I heard behind me a loud voice.** *In the Spirit* is where he received the greatest revelation of His life—one that has affected everyone who has ever named Jesus as Lord.

If you ever want to receive a revelation from God, if God is ever going to be real to you, you must learn the importance of being in this place called "in the Spirit." That is where everything God does in our lives is done.

Kenneth Hagin defines it this way: When you are in the Spirit, the things of God, beginning with His person, are more real, more eminent and more prominent in your life than things in the world.[2]

When you are in the Spirit, God and His Word and the things He talks about in His Word have a larger and more real place in your thinking and your life than the things in the natural world do. It is nothing "weird," or "flaky," or "far out."

Flowing in the Holy Spirit

It seems as if my wife, Lynne, has a vision or dream every other night or so. She hears the audible voice of God as well. It used to upset me when I would wake up in the morning and she would start telling me what "God said" to her. I would think, *I do not want to hear it. If God wants to talk to me, He can do it Himself.*

She would get wonderful revelation, and I was hearing nothing. I would pray, "God, You said You are no respecter of persons. But that does not seem to be true in my marriage. I am supposed to be pastoring my church, and I never hear from You! Supernatural events do not occur in my life as they do in hers. What is the deal?"

No answer.

I finally realized "the deal" was that Lynne was spending three-fourths of her life in the Spirit. She found that secret place and learned how to access it any time. So I began to put more of a premium on being in the Spirit. Then I began to experience more of God in my own life as well.

You can live by the Word, be blessed and prosper and still never experience the kind of things God wants to bring you when you are in the Spirit. That is the only way you can access those things. We have to learn where this place is and give it enough importance in our lives that we do the things the Bible says are necessary to experience it.

The only time in your life when everything is under your feet is when you are in heavenly places with Christ Jesus in the Spirit. If we are going to be spiritually equipped and brought to our highest level in God, we must learn how to get in the Spirit.

How To Begin in the Spirit

Assuming you are born again, your journey to learn how to be in the Spirit begins in Romans 8:6: **To be carnally minded is death, but to be spiritually minded is life and peace.** It begins with what you allow yourself to think. If you are filled with carnal thoughts, they minister to your flesh and make you mindful of the way the world thinks and acts.

You have to start being spiritually minded; you have to start thinking about God. You must begin thinking about God as you make an effort to get in the Spirit; you have to orient your thoughts toward the things of God.

This is what the apostle Paul meant when he talked about **bringing every thought into captivity to the obedience of Christ** (2 Cor. 10:5). It is not necessarily an easy step, but it is the first step.

Something which works for me is to start thinking about eternity; it draws me right into the Spirit. I am personally really excited about the things the Lord has shown me about eternity and the place we are all going to hold in it. When I think about these things, the things of this world become less real and begin to have less impact on me.

Lynne told me once that she would get in the Spirit by thinking of the Lord just holding her in His arms and cradling her. That never worked for me, but different people need different things to help them focus. For her it was comfort; for me it was excitement. Both worked just fine.

Focus your mind on God and the things in His Word that really minister to you, and you will start becoming spiritually minded. Our ability to do this is a prerequisite to accessing the Spirit.

Worship Into His Presence

Worship is another way we can experience being in the Spirit. **"God is Spirit, and those who worship Him must worship in spirit and truth"** (John 4:24). But it has to be in the Spirit. If you listen to someone singing a hymn and you raise your hands but your mind is out on the golf course, you are not worshipping in anything but your flesh. But when you focus your mind on God and begin worshipping Him in Spirit, you will be brought into the truth—the reality—of His presence.

> **What is the conclusion then? I will pray with the spirit, and I will also pray with the understanding. I will sing with the spirit, and I will also sing with the understanding.**
>
> **1 Corinthians 14:15**

This shows us that praying in the Spirit is different from praying in our understanding. If we do not understand what we are praying, then it is a mystery to our minds but not to our spirits.

Another way we access that place of being in the Spirit is to pray in other tongues. Singing in the Spirit, also known as singing in tongues, combines worship and praying in the Spirit.

You begin putting these things together—becoming spiritually minded, being a worshipper of God, praying in tongues, singing in the Spirit—and you will find the joy and peace of being in the Spirit. If you make this your fundamental approach to life and do not reserve it for your prayer closet or when you come to church, then being in the Spirit will start to feel like home.

When this becomes a pattern, you will become conscious of God throughout your day. I have heard it said that someone once asked Smith Wigglesworth how much he prayed each day. He replied that ten minutes was the longest he would ever pray but that he would not go ten minutes without praying.

Walking in the Spirit

Wigglesworth was conscious of abiding in God's presence every moment of his life. We can become so skilled in pressing through to the place of being in the Spirit that we do what the apostle Paul calls *walking in the Spirit.*

Walking in the Spirit means we are walking in the highest purpose of God and where His anointing is most present in our life. We are well able to meet whatever challenges we might encounter from the position of walking in the Spirit. Interestingly enough, it is also where we will get the greatest revelations from God. It is not coincidental that John recorded, **I was in the Spirit,** as the first thing he remembers about receiving the revelation from God.

CHAPTER FOUR

Your First Love

The first church the Lord addresses in John's revelation is the church at Ephesus. Ephesus was the capital city of the Roman province referred to as Asia; it was one of the largest cities in that part of the world. It was advantageously positioned at the confluence of several overland trade routes, two major rivers and the sea coast itself. An epicenter of commerce, Ephesus naturally became a large city.

Evangelizing the city of Ephesus was a challenge. The main temple of Diana, one of the seven wonders of the ancient world, was located there. Thousands of ardent followers made the city a center of idol worship. A very sensual, carnal kind of society grew up around this particular temple because of the sexual nature of the worship they engaged in.

But evangelize Ephesus they did! Church historians tell us the Ephesian church grew to over 10,000 members. For a church of those days, that was huge! More than that, it was viewed as being a spiritually mature church and very successful. It was one of the most notable works of the Lord in its day, and He commended them for their efforts.

For the most part, the churches in Asia were founded during Paul's second missionary journey, which began in A.D. 55. John wrote Revelation in A.D. 96, so at the time of the writing, the churches being addressed were about forty years old, or one generation.

The book of Ephesians, which Paul wrote to this church, demonstrates just how mature this body of believers really was. That particular epistle has to do with "in Christ" realities—truths which are not only for brand-new believers.

But in the intervening forty years much had happened to the Ephesian church, as we will see.

The Letter to Ephesus

"To the angel of the church of Ephesus write, 'These things says He who holds the seven stars in His right hand, who walks in the midst of the seven golden lampstands: I know your works, your labor, your patience, and that you cannot bear those who are evil. And you have tested those who say they are apostles and are not, and have found them liars; and you have persevered and have patience, and have labored for My name's sake and have not become weary.

'Nevertheless, I have this against you, that you have left your first love. Remember therefore from where you have fallen; repent and do the first works, or else I will come to you quickly and remove your lampstand from its place— unless you repent. But this you have, that you hate the deeds of the Nicolaitans, which I also hate. He who has an ear, let him hear what the Spirit says to the churches.

'To him who overcomes I will give to eat from the tree of life, which is in the midst of the Paradise of God.'"

Revelation 2:1-7

Jesus has many good things to say about the church at Ephesus, and He brings correction only after He has acknowledged the right things they have done. That is a good lesson for us today. If you want to correct somebody, then in order to ensure their receiving that correction in the spirit in which it is intended, first tell them you recognize and appreciate the *good things* they are doing.

"I Know Your Works"

Jesus said in verse 2, **"I know your works."** These are the works which resulted from their decision to believe and receive the Word of God and base their lives upon it. By faith, they put that Word to work in their lives. These were not dead works, or works done without faith, because Jesus would not have commended them for dead works.

He said they had labored for His name's sake. (v. 3.) The word *labor* connotes consistent, diligent effort. Faith is not quitting your job and floating around on a little cloud, waiting for the Lord to miraculously provide for you. That is mere stupidity; you and your family will starve to death.

The Word says we must be diligent in what we do and labor in what is good so we will have something to give to the needy. (Eph. 4:28.) The church at Ephesus made consistent, diligent effort in doing those things which emanate from a heart motivated by love and acting in faith.

Jesus also said the Ephesians were patient. That means they were consistent under pressure. They did not buckle when the going got tough; they were consistent in their stand on the Word of God under adverse circumstances. They were also doctrinally correct. They could not bear those who were evil, and they tested those who claimed to be apostles. They did not blindly follow.

Gnostics

Verse 6 says, **"You hate the deeds of the Nicolaitans, which I also hate."** Notice they did not hate the *Nicolaitans;* they hated their *deeds.* This was a cult, a sect of Gnostics who taught that God was only concerned with the spiritual realm and, therefore, it did not matter what we did in this natural life. They taught that there should be a community of wives, and there was no such thing in the physical body as adultery or fornication; those were only spiritual concerns.

The Ephesian church recognized this teaching as wrong and hated it, as Jesus did; and He commended them for that.

They understood the biblical truth that you know the proof of someone's call by the fruit that person produces (Matt. 7:20) and not by supernatural manifestations. A common problem in that day was that they confused the spectacular with the genuinely supernatural.

That is why Jesus said:

> **"Many will say to Me in that day, 'Lord, Lord, have we not prophesied in Your name, cast out demons in Your name, and done many wonders in Your name?'**
>
> **"And then I will declare to them, 'I never knew you; depart from Me, you who practice lawlessness!'"**
>
> Matthew 7:22,23

Perhaps most significantly of all, Jesus commends them for not growing weary. (Rev. 2:3.)

Galatians 6:9 instructs us:

> **And let us not grow weary while doing good, for in due season we shall reap if we do not lose heart.**

If you hang in there and keep doing the Word, you will eventually reap your harvest. If you do not quit, you win!

Nevertheless...

Jesus commended them for all the things which to us indicate a strong, spiritually mature church. But then He said, **"Nevertheless I have this against you, that you have left your first love"** (Rev. 2:4). The consequence for the church if they do not change their ways just chills me to the bone: **"I will come to you quickly and remove your lampstand from its place—unless you repent"** (v. 5).

All of the good things we do mean absolutely nothing if we leave our first love. So we have to learn what it really means to leave our first love, and then we must learn how to correct it. Whatever we do—children's or youth ministry, evangelism, Christian schools, singing in the choir, preaching, praying or studying the Word—none of it makes any difference whatsoever, as far as God is concerned, if we have left our first love. And His opinion is the only one which should count to us.

According to verse 5, if you leave your first love, "the lampstand" of your life will be removed from God's presence. In other words, it will cost you the presence of God. Ultimately, it will bring utter destruction to your life. We get so locked into a works mentality that we often neglect the most important concern of all—our personal relationship with Jesus, our first love.

The sad part is that the Ephesian church did not heed this message; they did not repent. Today, the city of Ephesus is nothing but a pile of ruins overrun by tourists. The mighty Ephesian church doesn't even exist there. This was the largest, most prosperous, most mature church in its day; but their end was utter destruction because they left their first love and never found their way back again.

What Does It Mean?

What does "leaving your first love" mean? *The Amplified Bible* gives us a little more insight.

> **"But I have this [one charge to make] against you: that you have left (abandoned) the love that you had at first [you have deserted Me, your first love]."**
>
> **Revelation 2:4** AMP

Since the relationship between Christ and His church is like a human relationship, think about the person who is *your* first love.

The first love in your life is not just an object of adolescent infatuation. It is not a relationship born out of convenience or personal necessity. When you fall head over heels in love, something happens to you. It changes your personality; you get a little crazy. For the first time, perhaps, you place what another person thinks ahead of what you do. You want to please another person more than yourself.

Up to that point, most of us are pretty self-oriented. But all of a sudden, we begin to have an overwhelming desire to please someone else to the point of total self-sacrifice. You cannot think or talk about anything else, and you do not want to be anywhere except in that person's presence.

True Love

If you have never experienced that, you have never fallen in love. Before I began dating my wife, Lynne, I never used to look in the mirror much, except to shave or to run a comb through my hair. But once I was truly in love, I began spending some serious time there, making sure everything was as good as it could be.

I never used to like to talk on the telephone. I thought it was a waste of time—until there was a little distance between my first love and me. Then I burned up the phone lines and ran up huge long-distance bills.

Your first love is such an intense thing that it begins to alter the way you view reality and change your priorities. That person becomes the primary focus of your life, and you are overwhelmed with a desire to be a blessing to him or her and to see that person's needs met.

Within this framework, I want you to understand how we can measure whether or not our first love is still in place. No Christian—especially if he or she is into works—wants to acknowledge it if Jesus does not hold the place of priority He used to.

They will lie to themselves and to others. They will put on a facade so no one will know Jesus has dropped into second place behind their families, their business or even their golf game. There are two main indicators which let you know whether Jesus holds the place in your life He should.

Passion

The first indicator is passion—or lack of it. There should be a passion for Jesus similar to what you feel for your first human love. Are you still consumed with a desire to please Him, to have your life be a blessing to Him, to spend more time in His presence? How much of your thought life does He occupy? When your mind is free, does it go to Him or other places? Is it more fun to talk about your hobby, your business, your day at the office or your favorite team?

You might think to yourself, *This fella is fanatical.* No, I am not. This is descriptive of how we act if we are relating to Jesus in the manner He wants. This is the way it should be for us. This is the kind of intensity we have to maintain.

There are people who cannot identify with this at all. They have never had this kind of passion for the Lord. Not ever. Yet the Lord said that if we do not love Him more than father, mother, husband, wife, sister or brother, then we are not worthy of Him. (Matt. 10:37.) He has to be first if we are going to be what He wants us to be and if we are going to experience a blessed life.

Dependence

The second indicator that you have left your first love is that you are no longer dependent upon Jesus as you once were. He is the Head of the church, the One to whom you should be submitted. He is entitled to be the Head of your life because He bought you with the price of His blood. Just as we are totally dependent on Him for salvation, so should we depend on Him in every single area of our lives.

Now, some of us are partially dependent. When we need healing, we depend on Him in that area.

We say, "I am doing fine with my finances, Lord; I am doing all right with my business, but my body needs healing. Heal me, Lord."

Or we say, "My relationship with my spouse is not very good; I need Your intervention there, God. But I don't need Your healing; I am handling my body just fine with diet, nutrition and exercise."

But it is utter, complete dependence on Him which keeps Him in the position of our first love. I remember when I first went into the ministry; I felt so inadequate, so out of place. As I look back on that time, I see it as a place of precious dependence on the Lord.

There was no question about it—I had no business being in the pulpit. I had no training for it; my college degree was in English, a pre-law curriculum. My experience in life had been as a pilot in the Air Force. I had no preparation at all for the ministry. "What am I doing here?" is something I can remember saying more times than once. "Lord, I am going to embarrass You—and me too. So how about we let somebody else do this?"

But when you are utterly dependent on Him, He can move; He can bring about His purpose with no interference. God does not need your *ability,* He desires only your *availability!*

Total and complete dependence on God for everything in our lives is necessary for His highest and best to be realized.

The problem in all of this is that, as He begins to use us because we are dependent upon Him, success and increase come; and because we have learned a few things, we start getting independent. We somehow imagine that we've gotten where we are because of something we've done.

The Word says that when we have been blessed by the Lord, we must take care not to forget that the Lord is the source of the blessing or we will eventually be destroyed. (Deut. 8:11-19.) That is the human tendency: We come to Him when there is a crisis, a time of need, and we depend on His goodness, grace and mercy. But as soon as He bails us out, we forget what He has done.

The Consequence

The Lord has to remove us from His presence when we do not keep Him as our first love. It has to be that way; we would abuse the anointing, twist the power and profane the glory that comes with His presence if we were not putting His will first.

Is the passion still there? Was it ever? Are you *completely* dependent upon Him? If the answer to any of these things after an honest self-examination is no, then the instruction to you is the same as it was to the church at Ephesus: Repent, or the lampstand of your life will be removed from the presence of God.

What happens then? You become a religious institution. You can raise your hands without raising your hands to God. You can pray without praying to God; many people do. You go through the motions, but your mind is somewhere else. It becomes a religious exercise to do the works without your heart being in them.

The Solution

So what do we do if the passion has subsided or if the dependence is no longer there? What do we do to get things going again?

On many occasions, we have heard a husband or wife say, "I do not love him (or her) anymore; the fire is gone. I am not sure I want to be in this relationship anymore."

The counsel I give such a person is the same as Jesus gave the church at Ephesus: **"Remember therefore from where you have fallen; repent and do the first works"** (Rev. 2:9). You have to do the first works if you are going to have the first love. In other words, start doing the works again that you did when you were first consumed with love, and it will rekindle the passion.

Many people make the mistake of waiting for the passion to come or expecting God to change them before they will do the works of love. That is backwards. When you do the works, it generates the passion.

Remember, **Delight yourself also in the Lord, and He shall give you the desires of your heart** (Ps. 37:4). According to *The American Heritage Dictionary*, the word *delight* means "to take your pleasure in, rejoice in, and focus your attention on."[1]

Initially, your works of love may be by faith. But as you take these steps and do the first works, it will rekindle your passion for your spouse.

I have seen this in countless couples we have counseled. When people come to us with this kind of commentary, we tell them to start acting as they did when they were madly in love with each other.

Do it by faith, but do the same things. Start telling her thirty-five times a day that you love her more than anything else on earth. Start sending her flowers, write cards and notes, open the door, pull out her chair, tell her she is beautiful.

A wife should be telling her husband he is the next best thing to Jesus, that he is the best-looking hunk she ever saw, that he is her knight in shining armor, that she respects him, that she loves him, honors him, defers to him.

I guarantee you the flame will be rekindled. I guarantee you the passion will be ignited. The intensity will be reborn, and your marriage will become what you and God want it to be.

A properly functioning marriage relationship is one of the greatest assets we can have toward maintaining our first love, Jesus. Marriage is a type of the relationship between Christ and His church; if your marriage is not in order, the primary example for your relationship with Jesus is nonfunctional.

Since marriage is a type of the relationship between Jesus and the church, it is no wonder that He said, **"Do the first works."** Think about Him; talk about Him; do those things that would be pleasing to Him; look for opportunities to be with Him in your prayer closet. Look for those things. Hunger for those things. Make yourself rejoice in Him.

It will cause your passion for God to burn hot once again, and the works you do will be the result of your genuine desire to do them. You will *want* to raise your hands in worship, give, go to church and pray. The fire of your life in God will be rekindled.

Reward to the Overcomer

"He who has an ear, let him hear what the Spirit says to the churches. To him who overcomes I will give to eat from the tree of life, which is in the midst of the Paradise of God."

Revelation 2:7

Overcome what? The specific challenge facing this church was to overcome the natural tendency of their flesh to abandon their first love.

We must overcome the distractions pulling us away from Him—even if they are good works—as important as they may be.

And out of the ground the Lord God made every tree grow that is pleasant to the sight and good for food. The tree of life was also in the midst of the garden, and the tree of the knowledge of good and evil.

Genesis 2:9

If we overcome and maintain our first love, Jesus will give us to eat of the Tree of Life; in other words, we will partake of the divine nature. This is the same opportunity Adam and Eve had in the Garden, but they chose to disobey instead.

This is not just life eternal, but also the quality of life Jesus came to give you now—freedom from sickness, disease, poverty and lack. Jesus promises that you will partake of the Tree of Life, of the divine nature, if you overcome the tendency to move away from Him, your first love. You will experience not only the timelessness of eternity, but also the God-kind of life *now*. He guarantees it, if you keep Him as your first love.

CHAPTER FIVE

The Persecuted Church

Smyrna was a beautiful little seacoast town on the Aegean sea. At the time of this letter, the city had been recently rebuilt by one of the generals serving under Alexander the Great. It was a gorgeous city, with wide boulevards and beautiful buildings, and it had become a resort town for wealthy Roman aristocracy.

As such, Smyrna had become a community on the leading social edge of the day. Because of its strong ties to Rome, spiritually and socially, it was a center for worshipping the Roman emperor. Emperor worship was at an apex of popularity at this time, and Smyrna was into it "lock, stock and barrel."

However, the church at Smyrna suffered great persecution because it opposed this practice. To her contemporaries the church at Smyrna was known as "the persecuted church."

**"And to the angel of the church in Smyrna write,
'These things says the First and the Last, who was dead,
and came to life: I know your works, tribulation, and
poverty (but you are rich); and I know the blasphemy of**

**those who say they are Jews and are not, but are a syna-
gogue of Satan. Do not fear any of those things which you
are about to suffer. Indeed, the devil is about to throw some
of you into prison, that you may be tested, and you will
have tribulation ten days. Be faithful until death, and I will
give you the crown of life. He who has an ear, let him hear
what the Spirit says to the churches. He who overcomes
shall not be hurt by the second death.'"**

Revelation 2:8-11

Jesus is addressing the challenge of persecution they faced. Even though much of the church world was experiencing persecution to one degree or another, Smyrna was immersed in that sad experience. They received the greatest portion of the persecution going on then.

We are not even remotely in the same boat with Smyrna; those people's lives were in jeopardy every day. Their experience has hardly any relevance to how we exercise our Christianity in America today. We simply do not know what persecution is. Because of that we take our faith too lightly, and we miss something important in our pursuit of the crown of life.

It Will Come

The first thing we need to know about persecution is that it is going to come: **Yes, and all who desire to live godly in Christ Jesus will suffer persecution** (2 Tim. 3:12).

Persecution is nothing more than being mocked or reviled by men. The results can be anything from verbal insults, to physical harm, to actual death. But it is coming against you for your faith, your belief in Jesus. There are always exceptions, but as a rule, in our society verbal persecution is about all you will suffer. Only recently have we seen people murdered for their faith here in America.

If you are not suffering at least some persecution, you are not living godly in Christ Jesus. If you are living for Jesus, somebody is going to have something to say about it. If that is not happening to you, you are too conformed to the world and not conformed enough to the image of Jesus. That's Bible.

Turn the Other Cheek

The second thing you need to know about persecution is that you need to turn the other cheek, not resist.

For many people, that concept simply does not compute. So let us clear up some of the misconceptions about turning the other cheek. Jesus' teaching is a good place to start.

> **And seeing the multitudes, He went up on a mountain, and when He was seated His disciples came to Him.**
>
> **Matthew 5:1**

The Sermon on the Mount was not a general address to everyone about how to live life; it was addressed to the disciples, the ones who were going to be taking the gospel into the world when Jesus left. He was teaching them how to conduct themselves as ministers of the gospel.

> **"Blessed are those who are persecuted for righteousness' sake, for theirs is the kingdom of heaven. Blessed are you when they revile and persecute you, and say all kinds of evil against you falsely for My sake. Rejoice and be exceedingly glad, great is your reward in heaven, for so they persecuted the prophets who were before you."**
>
> **Matthew 5:10-12**

> **"You have heard that it was said, 'An eye for an eye and a tooth for a tooth.' But I tell you not to resist an evil person. But whoever slaps you on your right cheek, turn the other to him also."**
>
> **Matthew 5:38,39**

Here we have a source of misunderstanding which has plagued the religious world for centuries and has caused many people to say, "I don't want any part of being a Christian if you have to let the world walk all over you."

This is ignorance gone to seed.

The Bible makes it clear that we are to resist the devil, the incarnation of evil, and he will flee from us. (James 4:7.) This sounds as if it contradicts what Jesus taught earlier (Matt. 5:39), unless you read that Scripture in context. Jesus is instructing His disciples about the conduct of ministry regarding persecution. When evil people come against you because of your stand for Jesus, you do not need to defend yourself; turn the other cheek.

Resist Evil

But on every other occasion when you confront evil which does not fall into the category of persecution for your faith, you are to strongly resist evil.

If someone breaks into your house and rapes your wife, are you going to turn the other cheek and offer him your daughter also? Get serious! You know you would not, and neither would I.

You resist evil in every way possible, *except* when you are being persecuted for the name of Jesus. This is true not only on an individual basis, but also on a corporate basis. As a country, we resist evil on a national level. God does not say we should not defend our nation, we should not fight or we should not kill.

"But, Mac, doesn't the Bible say, 'You shall not kill?'"

No, it does not! It says, **"You shall not murder"** (Ex. 20:13). As a matter of fact, Ecclesiastes 3:3 says there is a time to kill, and one of those occasions is when you're defending the nation where God has placed you.

Romans 13 says, **The authorities that exist are appointed by God** (v. 1), and that government **does not bear the sword in vain** (v. 4). This wimpy brand of Christianity which says you have to let the world walk all over you is straight from the pit of hell. This teaching chases people right out the back door. Who would want to be part of that?

Yet in all things we are more than conquerors through Him who loved us (Rom. 8:37). There are going to be occasions when you have to stand against evil with every conceivable tool at your disposal and resist it to the very core of your being, or the devil will run roughshod over you.

Very often, the people who say, "Peace, brother," are the same people who do not know the true meaning of turning the other cheek. When someone comes against what they believe, instead of turning the other cheek, they get offended, defensive and start arguing.

This is what it means to turn the other cheek: You simply love the persecutor, letting him see the light of God shining through you.

The most effective response to persecution that we will ever have in the name of Jesus is to smile, love persecutors and not defend ourselves. Let the Lord be your recompense and justification. Then He can use you to bring them into the kingdom. They will see something in you no one else has shown them: tolerance of criticism. Jesus does not need your defense. Besides, it is His reputation at stake, not yours.

Persecution Carries Great Reward

The third thing you need to know about persecution is that it carries great reward. When you are willing to be faithful *even to death*, Jesus said He would give you a crown of life.

Just because it is not likely to be necessary in our society today does not mean this is not typically a standard of measurement for us. We need to become determined in our hearts that we would be faithful even if it required our death. It is the only way we will inherit a crown of life.

And do not be so arrogant as to say, "I would never deny Jesus!" I can remember somebody named Peter who said that, and he walked with Jesus in the flesh, saw the miracles and felt the presence of Jesus in a way we cannot until we are in heaven. Yet he still denied Him three times. So be certain you make an accurate assessment of yourself. Are you willing to be faithful even to death?

The letter to Smyrna carries a very significant message for us today. Dealing with pressure brought on by adverse circumstances is going to be a necessity if we are ever to inherit the crown of life.

Poverty and Prosperity

**"I know your works, tribulation, and poverty (but you
are rich); and I know the blasphemy of those who say they
are Jews and are not, but are a synagogue of Satan."**

Revelation 2:9

Notice that poverty is identified here as an adverse circumstance, not
something God brings to you. But after mentioning their poverty, the Lord
reminds them, **"But you are rich."** You may be experiencing material
lack now because of your assignment in the earth or because you are part
of a church under great persecution, but never forget you are rich in
eternal things:

**"But lay up for yourselves treasures in heaven, where
neither moth nor rust destroys and where thieves do not
break in and steal. For where your treasure is, there your
heart will be also."**

Matthew 6:20,21

God may give some of us a call on our lives that temporarily makes it
impossible for us to experience the limitless prosperity which is His promise
to each of us.

If the Lord calls you to go up the Amazon River, turn left at the fourth
fork and disappear into the mountains somewhere to minister the gospel to
an obscure tribe, you cannot take your Cadillac, your checking account
and your wardrobe with you. If you are going to answer the call of God,
there will always be things you have to leave behind.

Does that mean it is not the will of God for you to prosper? No. It means
sometimes the way we are called prevents us from walking in the fullness
of prosperity *here on earth*.

But answer the call anyway, and you'll lay up treasure for yourself in
heaven. Do not forget: You are rich. You are rich in Jesus Christ. You will never
have a need which is not met.

The call of God always takes precedence. There are many people who
have fallen into a ditch because of the "prosperity" message; they will not

answer the call of God because it would limit what their material blessings could be. Do not fall into this trap.

One of the things Jesus was pointing out to the church at Smyrna was that it is not His will for us to experience poverty, which is why He said, **"But you are rich"** (Rev. 2:9). You have access to the source of all provision; do not forget that.

Those Who Are Not

Jesus continues in verse 9, **"...and I know the blasphemy of those who say they are Jews and are not, but are a synagogue of Satan."** Sadly, we will probably receive most of our persecution from those who say they are Christians but are not. These people adopt a value system other than the Bible, but they still call themselves Christians and are threatened by your stand on the Word of God.

The word *tribulation* in verse 9 is defined in *Strong's Exhaustive Concordance* as "pressure, persecution, or affliction."[1] *Affliction* is anguish or distress produced by the pressure of adverse circumstance.[2]

The enemy of your soul cannot deceive you if you know the Word of God. The only way he can keep you from being faithful is to pressure you. Pressure is intended to push you away from your committed stand for the Lord, causing you to be unfaithful and, therefore, to lose your crown of life.

Jesus is telling us prophetically that adverse circumstances are going to come for the church. Your challenge and mine is to remain faithful regardless of that pressure; then we will inherit a crown of life.

"Be faithful until death, and I will give you the crown of life" (Rev. 2:10). The word *life* in the Greek is *zoe*, "the God-kind of life, life as God has it."[3] The crown represents authority, rule and dominion. If you want God's kind of life, which incorporates dominion and authority over every adverse circumstance, you will have to learn how to be faithful no matter what the circumstances and pressures are.

Being Faithful

We must know what God defines as being faithful, and then we must become that.

Faithful means "loyal and devoted."[4] What does it mean to be faithful to God? It begins by being faithful to His Word. You cannot be faithful to God without being faithful to His Word; God and His Word are one.

His Word comes to us in two ways: the written Word in the Bible, which applies to everybody in general; and the word spoken to our hearts by the Holy Spirit—things about our giftings, our personalities and our calls which are unique to us.

If you are going to get a crown of life, you have to be faithful to God's Word, regardless of the form in which He gives it to you.

Do you say, "I have been faithful; I tithe; I go to church every Sunday. Why do I still lack dominion and authority over circumstances?"

Then I will ask, "Have you been faithful to what God has spoken to your heart? Were you faithful to share your faith with your neighbor last week, when you knew God put it on your heart to do so? Were you faithful to do that little thing for your husband or wife He told you to do, even though it meant humbling your heart?"

Those kinds of things come to bear on receiving your crown of life and the dominion He wants you to walk in just as much as obeying the written Word does.

Then is being faithful measured only by what you do? No. There are two other primary considerations regarding faithfulness: *what you think* and *what you say.* If you are unfaithful in either of these areas, you have no right to expect dominion over the circumstance producing the pressure.

You cannot be faithful with your words and your actions if you are not faithful in your heart and mind. Jesus said of the scribes and Pharisees, **"These people draw near to Me with their mouth, and honor Me with their lips, but their heart is far from Me"** (Matt. 15:8).

You can act like a good church-going Christian, be sweet to everybody and still be thinking bad thoughts about your neighbor and be angry, unforgiving, coveting and lustful.

Why do you think Paul said, **Casting down arguments and every high thing that exalts itself against the knowledge of God, bringing every thought into captivity to the obedience of Christ** (2 Cor. 10:5)? That is faithfulness.

Here is the bottom line from the letter to the church at Smyrna. You can overcome every circumstance standing in the way of God's will for your life—you can put on that crown of life, and the authority will carry you through every worldly pressure which comes along—as long as you are faithful to the Lord in what you think, speak and do. That may not be *easy*, but it is *simple*.

CHAPTER SIX

The Deceived Church

Pergamos was the political capital of the Roman province of Asia during John's time and was also a well-known cultural center of the day. Located approximately seventy-five miles north of Ephesus, the city had one of the best-known libraries in antiquity, with over 200,000 volumes. Pergamos was where parchment was first used. Intellectuals from all over the world, as well as Roman aristocrats, often gathered at Pergamos.

Because of the heavy Roman influence, as in Smyrna, the Pergamites were involved in Roman emperor worship. As with Smyrna, the church at Pergamos suffered persecution for refusing to participate in such idolatry. Jesus made reference to His faithful martyr Antipas.

"And to the angel of the church in Pergamos write, 'These things says He who has the sharp two-edged sword: I know your works, and where you dwell, where Satan's throne is. And you hold fast to My name, and did not deny My faith even in the days in which Antipas was My faithful martyr, who was killed among you, where Satan dwells.

'But I have a few things against you, because you have there those who hold the doctrine of Balaam, who taught Balak to put a stumbling block before the children of Israel, to eat things sacrificed to idols, and to commit sexual immorality. Thus you also have those who hold the doctrine of the Nicolaitans, which thing I hate.

'Repent, or else I will come to you quickly and will fight against them with the sword of My mouth.

'He who has an ear, let him hear what the Spirit says to the churches. To him who overcomes I will give some of the hidden manna to eat. And I will give him a white stone, and on the stone a new name written which no one knows except him who receives it.'"

Revelation 2:12-17

Deceived

The people of the church at Pergamos didn't deny their faith, even when their members were being martyred! But the Lord had something against them. They were deceived. The deception had not cost them their faith, but they were deceived nonetheless.

Jesus is talking about deception among believers who are committed to God, not those who are "weird," "strange" or "far out."

Let me define deception for you: Deception is failing to anchor your life on something other than the unchangeable Word of God and still expecting your future to be secure.

Many people believe that Jesus is the Son of God and that each of us has the need to be born again; they have based their lives upon that. But through willful ignorance or the influence of other deceived people, they have come to believe that God does not care about their healing or that He uses sickness to teach them a lesson or that He wants them to be poor.

The Lord makes it clear that He expects us not to continue in fellowship with people who are holding to some other doctrine. This is a hard thing for a lot of people to hear. It was a difficult thing for me to hear when all of my friends believed other things. They were a worldly bunch, and they did not believe much of what I had decided to base my life on.

I began to understand that if I was going to grow in God, I had to move away from fellowship with corrupt, worldly people who opened me to deception. I was either going to bring them into my belief or break the fellowship.

Do not be unequally yoked together with unbelievers. For what fellowship has righteousness with lawlessness? And what communion has light with darkness?

2 Corinthians 6:14

So what do we do about it?

Therefore "Come out from among them and be separate, says the Lord. Do not touch what is unclean, and I will receive you. I will be a Father to you, and you shall be My sons and daughters, says the Lord Almighty."

Therefore, having these promises, beloved, let us cleanse ourselves from all filthiness of the flesh and spirit, perfecting holiness in the fear of God.

2 Corinthians 6:17-7:1

The answer is to make an effort to bring them to a point of belief which will enable you to have fellowship with them; but if they refuse or resist, you must separate yourself from them. You do not have to be rude; just speak the truth in love. Your growth in God, your success in God and the blessing of God are dependent on it.

Forget the mentality which says, "I will 'infect' them with my holiness." It will never happen; rather, they will infect you with their unbelief. The book of Haggai makes it clear: **Holiness is not infectious…. Unholiness is infectious** (Hag. 2:12,13 AMP).

Unsaved Family

If the unbeliever with whom you have fellowship is a wife, husband or relative, you cannot abandon such a relationship. Because you have responsibilities and obligations in these relationships, God gives a different approach to them.

First Peter 3:1-7 gives us very clear instruction about a person who is joined by blood or by marriage to an unbeliever. He says you can win that unbeliever without preaching a word by your manner of life. You must, however, quit talking it and start living it; then your relatives will come into the things of God.

If you have not experienced success in ministering to loved ones, you are talking and arguing too much and not living it enough. When you live it out in front of them, you do not have to say a word.

I would not be serving God today if I had not seen the changes God made in my wife. She did not preach to me or condemn me; she just prayed for me and lived out the changes which were occurring in her heart. She loved me as she had never loved me before, reaching out to me in every way she possibly could. She would pray and ask God what she could do to convince me of His love for me and then speak blessings over me.

She never said a word to me about what she was doing. But I saw the change in her, and it made me want what she had.

If your unbelieving relatives or spouse ask you about the Word, certainly talk about it, but *never* argue it. Simply live it, and God will work through you to bring change in their lives. If they are stubborn, you may not see any change for a while, but something is happening in their hearts because His Word is true and *never* fails.

That does not mean, however, that you can fellowship with them in their deception. Separate yourself from fellowship with them in the area of their deception. When they want to do something wrong, you just say, "Honey, I am sorry, but I cannot do that. You know I love you, but you also know that goes against what I believe is right. So I am not going to do that with you. I love you, but I am not going to join in."

Then change the subject, and do not leave that area open for any further discussion.

We must evaluate the people we fellowship with, separating ourselves from those who are in deception. And if we cannot separate ourselves from the person because of blood relation or marriage, then we must separate ourselves from the area of deception they are involved in. This will close a major door to the devil.

Doctrine of Balaam

The church at Pergamos had wrongly continued in fellowship with two different forms of deception. The two common ways in which deception manifests in a believer who loves God are referenced by the terms "doctrine of Balaam" and "doctrine of the Nicolaitans." Jesus mentioned these as a way to reveal what the most common challenges may be for us in the area of deception in the church.

The "doctrine of Balaam" is a reference to a prophet of God. Balaam was an anointed man, a legitimate prophet to the children of Israel.

Israel was just coming out of their captivity in Egypt, moving three million strong toward the land of promise. But a people called the Moabites occupied the land. The Moabites had heard about the things God had already done on Israel's behalf, and they were frightened of the potential consequences for their way of life.

Balak, the king of Moab, was not particularly excited about engaging the children of Israel in battle because of all he had heard about their God, who fought on their behalf. So he decided to hire a prophet who would prophesy against Israel to bring a curse against them and undermine what the Lord was doing for them.

The king offered a great reward to Balaam; and while Balaam was smart enough to realize he could not make any proclamation, blessing or curse, except what was prompted by God, he wanted the reward very badly. So badly, in fact, that he used his office and knowledge to pursue the king's reward rather than to be obedient to God's leading. (Num. 22-24.)

Using the gifting of God for personal gain or reward, rather than being obedient to the direction of the Lord, is the deception of Balaam.

Using Your Gifting

You might be saying to yourself, "I am not a prophet or minister, so I do not have to worry about that." Not true. The giftings of God have been given to every man and woman—natural gifts and talents, intellectual capacities and spiritual giftings designed to bring you into the will of God for your life.

Do not think this is just happenstance. The Father has equipped you to do what He has planned for you to do; it is the gifting of God. God intends for you to use the fruit of that gifting for His purpose, not yours.

Our tendency, however, is to use our giftings to benefit or bless ourselves only and leave the Lord's purpose out. The most obvious example is probably the gift of money, but it could also be personal power, recognition, fame, success, achievements or even relationships.

God has given you the power to get wealth to establish His covenant (Deut. 8:18), and we find our greatest liberty with money when we do just that.

When you use your gifting to create wealth for yourself, rather than the purposes of God, you have fallen into the deception described here as the doctrine of Balaam.

The Lord does not expect you to live like a pauper. He will increase you when you are working for Him. But Jesus said, **"Seek first the kingdom of God and His righteousness, and all these things shall be added to you"** (Matt. 6:33).

God will increase you supernaturally when you make all your resources available to Him.

Another good way to measure whether the deception of Balaam is working on you is to evaluate how you make decisions about where you go and what you do. I have discovered the majority of people who love the Lord and want to do His will still have a tendency to make most of their decisions based on the profit motive.

No believer wants to admit that he has a priority other than God or that deception has touched his life. But understand this: If the prospect of reward or personal gain—rather than simple obedience to the Word and direction of the Spirit—is your basic consideration, then you are involved in deception.

The Doctrine of the Nicolaitans

I have already introduced you to this particular cult, but I want to focus on a specific doctrine they advocated. They elevated their clergy and certain holy men to places of high importance. According to their doctrine, no one—especially women—could get to God except through one of these men. Their doctrine taught there was no equality among believers.

The Bible teaches exactly the opposite. Paul makes the point time and again that we are all equal in Christ. Male or female, slave or free—it makes no difference; we are all equal in the eyes of God. (Gal. 3:28.) Some may be more prominent, but never confuse prominence with significance. Everyone has an equal shot at being significant in the kingdom of God. Even the most highly prominent people put on their pants one leg at a time just as you do and fight the same devil you fight on a daily basis, and they receive no special attention from God that is not also available to you.

The Nicolaitans directed people to look to men, instead of to God. Therein lies the other major root of deception.

The Bible says we are to be **looking unto Jesus, the author and finisher of our faith** (Heb. 12:2). Do not put your faith in man. Man will disappoint you, fail you and hurt you. And when one does, do not renounce your faith just because somebody fell! If you get a bad haircut, you do not quit getting haircuts; you just find another barber. But if you are focused on a person and have invested so much respect, admiration and esteem into that person, then if (or when) something happens to that person, it can be a devastating experience.

That is why the Bible says, **Recognize those who labor among you, and are over you in the Lord and admonish you, and to esteem them very highly in love for their work's sake. Be at peace among yourselves** (1 Thess. 5:12,13).

It is the ministry *office* which is to be esteemed, not the man. Confusing the two is a doorway to deception. Nearly all Christian persuasions have some of their doctrine right and some wrong. Why is that? Because they decided to look to man, to clergy, to church tradition, instead of to the Word of God.

Protecting Against Deception

How can I be sure I am not in deception? The first test question is, "Am I anchored in the Word of God?" Measure everything you decide to do by the Word. Don't do anything casually; think about it and ask yourself, "Will I violate a principle of the Word?" The Holy Spirit is there in your heart, and if you listen to Him, He will show you. Train yourself.

Secondly, there are decisions you have to make when God speaks to you directly by His Holy Spirit. How do you know you are not being deceived? How do you know it is really the voice of the Holy Spirit and not just your flesh? Again, measure it by the Word taken in context. Do not pull out one or two phrases and say, "The Word says it is okay." If you want to do something contrary to a principle in the Word, then it is not the Holy Spirit.

Thirdly, there are those occasions where the Word does not address a certain thing you want to do which doesn't violate a principle; but you wonder whether it is the right thing to do or a ploy of the devil to get you off track.

The desire God plants in your heart is the primary way the Holy Spirit will lead you in your life. We call this deep desire "the inward witness." It is confirmation on the inside of you that something is right.

Now, desire originates in two places: in your flesh, as lust, and in your spirit. If you will do what Psalm 37:4 says and **delight yourself also in the Lord,** then the desires you develop will be a revelation of God's will and you will not be deceived. When you delight yourself in the Lord, He reveals to you the next step in His will for your life. Then you can walk down that path with confidence and boldness.

Wrongly Connected

If you are not deceived but are in fellowship with people who are, how do you approach them? Do you just slam the door on them? If they are in ministry, do you expel them from the ministry? What do you do when somebody among you is in deception?

Galatians 6:1 instructs us:

> **Brethren, if a man is overtaken in any trespass, you who are spiritual restore such a one in a spirit of gentleness, considering yourself lest you also be tempted.**

We must make a strong effort to restore. If someone is on the wrong track, we do not let him ride it off the cliff, possibly taking others with him without even knowing it. Rather, we are to approach him with understanding, knowing that we are not so spiritual and intelligent that it could never happen to us. This is what it means to go to such a person in meekness.

If he will hear us, then restoration can come and we do not lose the valuable fellowship God desires. However, if he does not respond to the corrective effort of the Holy Spirit through us, then we have no choice but to do what Romans 16:17-18 says:

> **Now I urge you, brethren, note those who cause divisions and offenses, contrary to the doctrine which you learned, and avoid them. For those who are such do not serve our Lord Jesus Christ, but their own belly, and by smooth words and flattering speech deceive the hearts of the simple.**

Now, this Scripture does not advocate a public marking. God never humiliates anybody in public; that is not the way He works.

But we *should* mark those who are deceived among us. The word *mark* simply means "to take note of."[1] We are to take note of people who fall in this category and take responsibility for our own lives by avoiding them.

The Hidden Manna

> **"To him who overcomes I will give some of the hidden manna to eat. And I will give him a white stone, and on the stone a new name written which no one knows except him who receives it."**

> **Revelation 2:17**

What is the hidden manna? Manna is a type of the Word of God. As manna fed the Israelites in the wilderness, the Word of God spiritually feeds us now. Jesus said we had no need of the literal manna received by the forefathers, because He is now our Bread of Life. (John 6:31-35.) The Word is our manna, and Jesus is the Word; therefore, Jesus is our manna.

So, what is the *hidden* Word? It is the Word the Holy Spirit speaks to you directly. First Corinthians 2:7 calls it **the hidden wisdom**—things our eyes have not seen, nor our ears heard.

But this wisdom remains hidden from you until you have taken care of any deception that keeps you from establishing your life on the Word of God. If you have been deceived and away from the written Word, then you are not going to have the hidden manna.

The White Stone

Then Jesus says something most unusual in Revelation 2:17. He says, **"I will give him a white stone...."** In the first century, a white stone was a symbol of being acquitted by a court of law. In those days a judge had two stones—a white one and a black one. The black stone meant a guilty judgment; a white stone meant acquittal.

We know we have already been forgiven of our sins by the Father because of the blood of Jesus, so why do we need acquittal?

Well, sin is not our only problem. Sin produced something called the curse. The curse in the earth today has brought everything from sickness to poverty and wars.

I used to wonder why I saw people who were born again and loved God, yet still seemed to live under the curse. They were still sick or poor or dealing with problems with their spouses or children. Why were they still battling these curses?

They were deceived. They did not know God would heal them or prosper them or that in Christ they could do all things or that they were more than conquerors. Their deception was keeping the hidden manna from their lives.

But the reward for overcoming deception is a white stone: acquittal from the curse which surrounds this planet.

The new name written on the stone, which no man knows except the recipient, is indicative of a new life.

You can be born again without experiencing a bit of change in your life. You can still be without vision and have the curse all around you. You can know you are going to heaven but still not have a new life.

However, as you overcome deception—ground your life on the truth of the Word, sever those relationships with people who are in darkness and begin doing what you know you need to do—you are acquitted from the curse. God opens the hidden manna to you and reveals His plan for your life and, like Abram of old, you step into a new life with a new name.

CHAPTER SEVEN

The Worldly Church

T hyatira was located on the Lycus river, thirty-five miles southeast of
Pergamos. It was founded by one of Alexander the Great's generals.
Manufacturing wool and dyeing fabric were their main trades, along with
weaving, pottery and metalworking. Lydia, the seller of purple in Acts, was
a native of Thyatira. The madder root and local waters were essential to
the quality of the dyeing process.

Thyatira had highly organized trade and craft guilds, which were the
forerunners of the modern unions of today. You could say it was a "union
town" but with one big difference: The trade guilds in Thyatira also strongly
promoted particular forms of pagan rituals and worship. Gainful employ-
ment in the city was dependent on belonging to one of these guilds. And
to belong to the guild, you had to follow their particular form of idol worship.

Christians who lived in Thyatira were under a lot of pressure to involve
themselves in pagan practices just to have jobs. The end result was that
the church members began to lapse into sin, eating things sacrificed to
idols and committing fornication and other sexual sins.

The church at Thyatira is said to be one of the least significant of the seven churches, yet Jesus had more to say to this church than any other. He said:

**"And to the angel of the church in Thyatira write,
'These things says the Son of God, who has eyes like a flame
of fire, and His feet like fine brass: I know your works, love,
service, faith, and your patience; and as for your works, the
last are more than the first.**

**'Nevertheless I have a few things against you, because you
allow that woman Jezebel, who calls herself a prophetess, to
teach and seduce My servants to commit sexual immorality
and to eat things sacrificed to idols. And I gave her time to
repent of her sexual immorality, and she did not repent. Indeed
I will cast her into a sickbed, and those who commit adultery
with her into great tribulation, unless they repent of their
deeds. I will kill her children with death, and all the churches
shall know that I am He who searches the minds and hearts.
And I will give to each one of you according to your works.**

**'Now to you I say, and to the rest in Thyatira, as many
as do not have this doctrine, who have not known the depths
of Satan, as they say, I will put on you no other burden. But
hold fast what you have till I come.**

**'And he who overcomes, and keeps My works until the
end, to him I will give power over the nations—'He shall
rule them with a rod of iron; they shall be dashed to pieces
like the potter's vessels'—as I also have received from My
Father; and I will give him the morning star. He who has an
ear, let him hear what the Spirit says to the churches.'"**

Revelation 2:18-29

Jezebel

The key to understanding this letter is the name of the person referred to in verse 20: Jezebel. This is not a casual reference. Jezebel was the wife of Ahab, king of Israel. She was the daughter of another king, and Jezebel and Ahab's was a political marriage for the sole purpose of expanding the borders of Ahab's kingdom. But the marriage only compromised, or adulterated, the house of God with a kingdom of the world.

The church at Thyatira was the worldly church that compromised its integrity by pursuing worldly ideas and associations, inviting the world into the church.

In a nutshell, King Ahab's problem was exactly that. He deliberately joined the kingdom of God to a kingdom of the world through marriage in order to bring into the house of God the things he coveted in the world.

When you read about Ahab and Jezebel (1 Kings 16:31-22:40), you will discover their union produced the same results we see in Thyatira: fornication, idol worship and prophets of Baal.

But those sins are not the thrust of the Lord's address. They really are not the problem but rather the fruit of a deeper problem: association with the world. Falling into sin is the fruit of a worldly church.

The Worldly Church

Becoming a worldly church is a deadly thing. It is not easy to spot, and once it has touched your life, it becomes more difficult to eliminate. Worldly association is also the way the door is opened to seducing spirits.

Verse 20 says Jezebel, who represents the church's association with the world, not only teaches but seduces the church into these sinful practices. The primary opening to the deceiving and seducing spirits which work on Christians is too much love for the things of the world. This is the root cause of much of the sin we find in the church. James 4:4 explains:

> **Do you not know that friendship with the world is enmity with God? Whoever therefore wants to be a friend of the world makes himself an enemy of God.**

The consequence of Jezebel's sin is in verse 22, in which Jesus says He will **"cast her into a sickbed, and those who commit adultery with her into great tribulation, unless they repent of their deeds"** (Rev. 2:22).

This is not a reference to literal adultery. Rather, it is talking about the church getting into bed with the world: spiritual adultery. We are the bride of Christ, and when we begin to embrace the priorities and values the world holds, we have committed spiritual adultery. Jesus said we would experience great tribulation until we repent.

Verse 23 says, **"I will kill her children with death...."** Now, God is not going to be killing babies. We have to keep this in the context of spiritual adultery. When the church gets into bed with the world, the children the church produces will be spiritually dead. You cannot generate the life of God in your offspring if you are in spiritual adultery. If you have embraced the world to produce life, your children are going to be spiritually dead.

However, Jesus says in verse 26 that there is a significant reward for overcoming this temptation and for keeping His works to the end: **"...to him I will give power over the nations."**

Here is the deal: You are either going to be influenced by the world, or you are going to be an influence on the world. If you let the world into your life by compromise, you sacrifice your own authority.

But if you overcome this temptation, then you **"'shall rule them with a rod of iron; they shall be dashed to pieces like the potter's vessels'— as I also have received from My Father"** (v. 27). Jesus is talking about dominion: You will have dominion, power and authority over the world and the world's system. God's way will triumph in the situations of your life if you have kept the world out.

One of the ways we compromise is by being a little less radical, a little more touchable, a little more reachable for those elements of our society which have resisted the gospel and us in the past.

That is usually the rationale. We modify—dilute, or water down—our position on the Word of God to accommodate these different varieties of unbelief and sin.

This is opening the church door to the sin of the world, and it will cost us dearly. We will have great tribulation, and the offspring of that spiritual adultery will be spiritually dead.

Keeping the World Out

There are two ditches, or extremes, people fall into. The first is having no discernment whatsoever. If you do not use any discernment, your kids will be exposed to influences which will open them to sinful lives filled with pain and heartache.

The other ditch is just as bad. If you never go anywhere or take advantage of any of today's technology or take any pleasure in anything, you are setting your children up for a huge attack of their souls by the enemy. God has given us all things richly to enjoy. (1 Tim. 6:17). Do you think all the things which are a blessing to the world are just for the secular population? No.

Where do we draw the line? How do we distinguish between a right and wrong association? How do we go about our lives without living in fear of something "getting on us" or of being "corrupted" by something and still enjoy the things God has given us to enjoy?

Insulate with the Word; don't just isolate from the world. You need to get your priorities in the right order. Seek first the kingdom of God, and the good things of the world will be given to you.

Seducing spirits will say, *Come here. Do this. You can do that. A little is okay. No one will know. Why deny yourself? You are a good person. God will forgive you.* And we let ourselves believe them.

How, then, do we define our relationship to the world, our families and the church? Is there a way to keep out of the two ditches we mentioned?

Yes. The key is in the Word.

> **Do not love the world or the things in the world. If anyone loves the world, the love of the Father is not in him. For all that is in the world—the lust of the flesh, the lust of the eyes, and the pride of life—is not of the Father but is of the world. And the world is passing away, and the lust of it; but he who does the will of God abides forever.**
>
> **1 John 2:15-17**

God does not mind your having things, but He does not want you to give yourself to the pursuit of them. If you do, the love of the Father is not in you. You can have only one love: It is either the world or God.

The anointing of God will not be available to you if you love the world or the things in the world. You will be left solely to your own abilities. You will have no help from God.

Because the spirit of the world carries with it the spirit of antichrist, if we give ourselves to the pursuit of the world and the spirit of it, the love of the Father is not in us, and the anti-anointing will be our reward.

Most of us define our relationship with the world in terms of what we don't do. This is an unhealthy approach. Now, this does not mean you can do whatever you want; I am not suggesting you should throw away your common sense and the leading of the Holy Spirit.

But, I have heard people say they go to R-rated movies and plead the blood over them. "I am believing the profanity will not touch us," they say. "We will be able to look right over it. I am mature enough that those love scenes will not bother me. I want to see this movie, so I will simply ignore the bad parts."

Do not fool yourself! Use the common sense God gave you. If you expose yourself to that kind of trash, it will infect you; unholiness is always infectious. You have to use discernment.

Enjoying This World

We should be able to enjoy this world. I want my children and grand-children to have Disneyland, Christmas trees, presents and Easter egg hunts without being so bound up in this warped idea of removing ourselves from the world that they cannot enjoy anything.

So how do we enjoy the world without being influenced or affected by it? If we know that to love the world means the love of the Father is *not* in us, then we could turn that around and say that if the love of the Father *is* in us, the love of the world will *not* be.

Rather than focusing solely on what we have to withdraw from, we have to also focus on what we need to move toward—the love of the

Father. We need to focus on what we are becoming in Jesus, rather than what we are leaving in the world.

This simplifies the challenge of how to relate to the world. You do not need to back off in fear from everything you might want to do or every place you might want to go.

Use discretion, common sense and, most of all, the leading of the Holy Spirit. The wholesome things of the world can be enjoyed. Remember, fun is God's idea. If your motivation in life is to serve His purpose, you can enjoy those things to the fullest.

If we want to resist the spirit of the world and avoid the problems of the church at Thyatira, then we have to cultivate a heart to touch people with the love of Jesus and the Word of God. This has to become our priority. It has to become our reason for living.

Sadly, for most people, it is not. We might as well be honest and blunt about it. For most people (and I am talking about Christians here) their reason for living is their ministry, their bank account, their family or the next new toy.

Intellectually, they know they are supposed to be a light to the world and the salt of the earth, but when you get down to priorities, most people have an agenda that puts influencing their world somewhere down around the bottom of the list.

There are a lot of contributing factors to this, not the least of which is the basic tendency we all have to be more concerned about ourselves than anybody else.

But once we begin to respond to the heart of God, asking Him to give us a heart for people, we will gain a compassion for them and a desire to show them the way God sees them. Then we will begin to move away from self-concern to concern for others.

Influencing Our Communities

The other challenge to most people is to take up the banner of influencing their communities. To *evangelize* simply means "to spread the Good News, the gospel."[1] That is how we influence the world we live in.

Unfortunately, there is such a stereotype of the evangelist in most Christian circles that many people never become real participants in the process of spreading the Good News. We usually think, *I do not want to be a guy on a soap box, preaching on the corner, waving a Bible or knocking on doors. I just can't do that!*

Yes, there is such a thing as confrontational evangelism. You can see it in Acts 2; Peter preached a very fiery sermon on the Day of Pentecost. In verse 36, he basically told the crowd, "You crucified God"; and when they heard it, **they were cut to the heart** (v. 37), and thousands were saved.

If you are anointed and called to this ministry, it will flow naturally from you. You will not have to work at it, nor will it be a threat to you; on the contrary, it will give you great joy and excitement.

But not everyone is called to be a confrontational evangelist. So, how else can we influence our world? In the pages of the Bible, we find there are numerous styles and forms of winning people to Jesus.

As we briefly explore these various styles of evangelism, be on the lookout for the one that best fits your personality and temperament.

Persuasive Evangelism

In Acts 17:16-17, we find Paul displaying his flexibility and creativity in the area of evangelism.

Now while Paul waited for them at Athens, his spirit was provoked within him when he saw that the city was given over to idols. Therefore he reasoned in the synagogue with the Jews and with the Gentile worshipers, and in the marketplace daily with those who happened to be there.

That word *reasoned* in the Greek can be said to mean "disputed."[2] Did you know that it is not wrong to persuade somebody to receive Christ? Many believers came to Christ because of a well-reasoned, persuasive argument.

Many Christians have the mind-set which says, "If I just tell them they need Jesus, the anointing will do the rest." No. There are people who have to be persuaded; they are not going to come in any other way.

Paul was a well-educated man, and he reasoned with these people on an intellectual level and persuaded them. There is nothing more logical than the gospel. How illogical is the secular belief which teaches you came from a primordial sludge which evolved on its own into fish, then monkeys and then humans? You may be like Paul and persuade and reason with others so they can see the truth of the Word.

Lifestyle Evangelism

In Mark 5, we have the account of the maniac of the country of the Gadarenes. Jesus cast out the demons which were torturing him, and this man was so grateful that he wanted to go with Jesus.

And when He got into the boat, he who had been demon-possessed begged Him that he might be with Him. However, Jesus did not permit him, but said to him, "Go home to your friends, and tell them what great things the Lord has done for you, and how He has had compassion on you."

And he departed and began to proclaim in Decapolis all that Jesus had done for him; and all marveled.

Mark 5:18-20

There may be times to confront and other times to reason and persuade. But there are also times to testify to friends who know you (and know just how bad you used to be) about the great things God has done in your life.

God does not want you to alienate your friends by telling them they are going to burn in hell or by acting spiritually superior to them; that will just push them away. He wants you to live your life in such a way that they can see the change the Lord has made in you. Then when you say, "Look what the Lord had done for me," they will listen.

Service Evangelism

At Joppa there was a certain disciple named Tabitha, which is translated Dorcas. This woman was full of good works and charitable deeds which she did.

Acts 9:36

Dorcas was known by all because of the things she did for others. A wonderful way to influence people is to serve them. Take those new neighbors a pan of muffins or a pie. Serve a practical need; bless them.

When you serve people, their hearts open up to you. It makes them want to say, "Thank you, I appreciate what you did. Where are you from? Where do you work?" It opens the door to a very natural sharing of your life with God and an invitation to believe on Jesus.

Now, the first time they ask you where you live, do not say, "Get saved, or you will go to hell!" No. The more you serve them, the more open they become. It may take some time before their hearts are open enough to ask you something as intimate as a spiritual question can be. But as they see your willingness to serve them, they will be more willing to receive your message.

Here is an example. A young pastor started a new church in a very small community up north, where they get a lot of snow. The church bought him a truck with a plow on the front to plow out the church parking lot, and he decided one morning to plow out some of the houses closest to the church. As he did, he would leave a card with the name of the church and the words "Come see us sometime" on the back.

Every time it snowed, he would plow all the driveways in a three- or four-block radius and leave the little notes on the garage doors. That is all he did! The church grew to several hundred, built solely on the basis of shoveling other people's snow.

Invitational Evangelism

In John 4, we have the account of the Samaritan woman who met Jesus at the well. He told her things about herself that no one but the Son of God could have known.

The woman then left her waterpot, went her way into the city, and said to the men, "Come, see a Man who told me all things that I ever did. Could this be the Christ?"

Then they went out of the city and came to Him.

And many of the Samaritans of that city believed in Him because of the word of the woman who testified....

John 4:28-30,39

This is often called invitational evangelism. You may have difficulty exercising a great deal of influence on a personal level or even feeling comfortable sharing your faith for one reason or another, but one of the easiest ways is to invite somebody to come to church.

The Samaritan woman invited her whole city to come to Jesus. And they did. Environment can influence someone. (It works in the world all the time!) Why not invite them to the kind of environment in which God can bring His influence to bear in their lives?

Having a heart for people can revolutionize the worldly church.

CHAPTER EIGHT

The Traditional Church

Sardis was the capital of the province of Lydia, and it was probably the wealthiest city in all of Asia Minor. Coins were first minted in Sardis, and it had a thriving carpet industry. Located on the hills about thirty miles south of Thyatira and inland from Pergamos, Sardis was thought to be impregnable. But in 546 B.C., Cyrus the Great conquered Sardis by means of a secret route up a nearby cliff and carried away as much as one billion dollars' worth of gold and silver.

Sardis had an admirable name all over the world as a rich, desirable city with a well-established, wealthy church. But by the time the book of Revelation was written, the city had become decadent. They had grown used to being wealthy, and complacency had smothered them in their traditions. Jesus declared of them, **"You are dead,"** and **"I have not found your works perfect before God"** (Rev. 3:1,2).

Here is the letter He sent to the church at Sardis:

"And to the angel of the church in Sardis write, 'These things says He who has the seven Spirits of God and the seven stars: I know your works, that you have a name that

you are alive, but you are dead. Be watchful, and strengthen the things which remain, that are ready to die, for I have not found your works perfect before God. Remember therefore how you have received and heard; hold fast and repent. Therefore if you will not watch, I will come upon you as a thief, and you will not know what hour I will come upon you.

'You have a few names even in Sardis who have not defiled their garments; and they shall walk with Me in white, for they are worthy. He who overcomes shall be clothed in white garments, and I will not blot out his name from the Book of Life; but I will confess his name before My Father and before His angels. He who has an ear, let him hear what the Spirit says to the churches.'"

Revelation 3:1-6

In all of the other letters, works were mentioned in a good light. Sardis was the only church whose works He referred to negatively. They were doing good things, but the good works were imperfect in the eyes of God.

James gives us the essential clue why this was so:

Thus also faith by itself, if it does not have works, is dead.

James 2:17

The key part of that phrase is **by itself.** If it takes faith plus works to produce the life of God, and faith alone cannot do it, then it would be accurate to say works alone cannot do it either. Works which do not emanate from a heart of faith are dead.

Why would someone do something which does not come from his or her heart just to be doing it? I can answer that with a single word: tradition! Tradition is the real reason people do things they really do not have a heart to do.

Sardis was the "traditional church." The good works Sardis did, they did because "that is what a good church should do," but their hearts were not in them. This was why their works were not perfect, or complete; they were not mixed with faith.

The Danger of Tradition

Take a look at what Jesus said about tradition:

> **Then the Pharisees and scribes asked Him, "Why do Your disciples not walk according to the tradition of the elders, but eat bread with unwashed hands?"**
>
> **He answered and said to them, "Well did Isaiah prophesy of you hypocrites, as it is written: 'This people honors Me with their lips, but their heart is far from Me. And in vain they worship Me, teaching as doctrines the commandments of men.' For laying aside the commandment of God, you hold the tradition of men—the washing of pitchers and cups, and many other such things you do." He said to them, "All too well you reject the commandment of God, that you may keep your tradition."**
>
> **Mark 7:5-9**

Religious tradition makes people do things their hearts are not in. That is precisely what a hypocrite is—a person steeped in tradition who does things to be seen as someone who he or she really is not. This posturing, or image maintenance, is an essential part of traditional behavior.

But it comes at a terrible price:

> **"Making the word of God of no effect through your tradition which you have handed down. And many such things you do."**
>
> **Mark 7:13**

Now, that should really hit home. Nothing in the Bible will make the Word of no effect, but dead tradition will.

Tradition, as it relates to doing the works of God, cannot occur outside the context of religion. The instruction to the church of Sardis was given within a religious framework. The religious leaders of Jesus' day knew the Scriptures better than anyone else. And they should have known that Jesus is the Son of God, but they missed Him, primarily because they were overly religious and locked into tradition. (Luke 19:42-44.)

Many people do not know how poisonous religion can be. I hear this comment frequently: "I am a religious person." And people say it as though it were a good thing, something to be excited about.

Jesus fought the religious traditionalism of His time almost on a daily basis. He did not come to condemn the sinners, the tax collectors and the thieves; on the contrary, He made them His disciples. But virtually every time He encountered the religious leaders, His words to them were hard:

"Woe to you, scribes and Pharisees, hypocrites! For you are like whitewashed tombs which indeed appear beautiful outwardly, but inside are full of dead men's bones and all uncleanness."

Matthew 23:27

Dealing With Life

What is religion, and how does it become a part of our lives?

I believe it goes all the way back to the moment Adam's fellowship with God was broken. In Genesis 3:10, when Adam heard the voice of God, he was afraid because of his sin and hid from God.

The awareness of God's presence produces fear in the heart of a person who does not know God or is out of fellowship with Him. And there are really only three ways a person can deal with this fear, other than with the Word.

The first way is *materialism*. You immerse yourself in the world and distract yourself from the possibility that there is a God to whom you are going to have to give an account someday. The more you get into the world's ways, the less you have to think about the hollow place inside you that only God can fill and the less you have to deal with the possibility of having to account for your life to a higher authority.

The second way people deal with this fear is *denial*. This is called atheism. The theory says, "If I insist hard enough that there is no God, then maybe there really will not be one." The problem with this approach is that it still does not eliminate the anxiety about one's ultimate accountability nor the personal emptiness which can never be filled by anyone other than God.

The Downward Spiral of Religion

The third method of holding off the fear is to become *religious*. Religion builds a set of rules to appease a distant, angry God. It says, "If I do these things, but not those, that should make this distant, angry God happy with me. Maybe I can build some spiritual equity with Him if I behave properly."

Religion builds a set of rules to address the guilt we feel because we know there is a God, but we do not know Him or serve Him. The big problem with this strategy is that you cannot keep the rules. No one can. You cannot discipline human flesh to behave in a way that is pleasing to God. It takes the indwelling presence of the Holy Spirit to accomplish that.

Because people cannot keep religion's rules, they have more guilt, and so they build some more rules to deal with the new guilt. But they cannot keep them either. More guilt gets piled on the old guilt over and over again, leading them through a downward spiral.

Religion likes to pretend it is possible to keep the rules. Nobody will admit it is impossible. They have to keep trying harder and harder to keep these rules. They have to keep up appearances, so they pretend that when they reach a certain point of spirituality, they can keep all the rules.

The next step they take is to become proud of keeping the rules, which they are actually only pretending to keep. They have now exchanged a relationship with God for a religious fantasy. Now it would be a pretty tough pill to swallow if they took an honest look at the vicious cycle they are in.

But having committed to this course, religion then begins to look down on others who are not participating in this fantasy. Wars have been fought in the name of religion because of this. "You do not keep our rules, so you are not as good as we are; you do not accept our fantasy, so we are going to kill you."

Finally, as they become proud of pretending so well to keep the rules they know they are not keeping, the guilt gets unbearable. But they do not dare tell anybody because if they did, that person would know they were not keeping the rules.

It Only Seems Right

Religion is a despicable thing. You might ask yourself, "How in the world can humanity fall into this terrible, vicious trap?" Proverbs 14:12 explains: **There is a way that seems right to a man, but its end is the way of death.**

It is so easy to think you have to work for God's approval. After all, you have to work to earn a living. You have to work hard to succeed in life. We are taught a work ethic from childhood. It almost seems right that you should have to work to earn God's approval.

The rules of religion *seem* right, but they are not. Religion is a sad thing—something Jesus came to expose. He came to confront it, to show people what it really is and to tell them, "This is not the Father's will."

Tradition can be seen as the product of our effort to do things which will build spiritual equity with God to make Him happy with us. But as we can see from the Word, it is something which makes the Word of God of no effect.

The American Heritage Dictionary defines *tradition* as "a mode of thought or behavior followed by a people continuously from generation to generation."[1] As it relates to our pursuit of God, that "mode" comes to us principally from religion, or our effort to do things to appease God, rather than from our hearts.

Shape Shifter

He answered and said to them, "Well did Isaiah prophesy of you hypocrites, as it is written: 'This people honors Me with their lips, but their heart is far from Me. And in vain they worship Me, teaching as doctrines the commandments of men.'"

Mark 7:6,7

Tradition takes two different shapes. It can take the shape of a *doctrine.* Or it can be *a commandment of man* which is being taught as a doctrine of God but which cannot be found in the Word of God.

For example, infant baptism is not found in the Bible; it is a command-ment of men taught as a doctrine of God. The idea that you can be sprinkled as an infant and have the assurance of eternity in heaven is absolutely ludi-crous. It is not in the Word of God anywhere. You have to wonder how many countless millions of people have gone to hell because they grew up think-ing, *I was sprinkled when I was a baby. I do not need this "born again" stuff.*

This is one of the ways tradition robs the Word of God of its effective-ness: You are raised hearing a doctrine validated by the organization you are a part of and you are taught that it is true; then you close your mind to the Word of God in that area.

Do not believe what you hear from any pastor, rabbi, priest or minister—including this one—unless you can confirm it in the Word of God. That is the only way to be sure you are not engaging in a commandment of man.

However, a ministry which preaches the Word is not going to be holding on to the commandments of men, so that is not normally how tradition can enter. Those people are more susceptible to the other shape which tradition takes. Jesus describes it in verse 6: **"This people honors Me with their lips, but their heart is far from Me."** This is what Jesus had against the Sardis church.

I am convinced this is one of the reasons many people never experience the provision, blessing and power of God. Even though they go through the motions, they are doing it to please their spouses or a distant God whom they do not yet know. They feel guilt or condemnation, or they want to keep up appearances. They are not honoring God because the desire to do so burns in their hearts. They are doing it because it is doctrine, not desire.

Activate Your Faith

Nothing comes to us except by faith. It is only faith which bridges those impossible gaps and moves mountains. Only faith pleases God, and faith only comes by the Word of God, not by tradition. The way you solve the problem of tradition is by aligning the desires of your heart with God's Word.

If you do not like raising your hands, paying your tithes and giving offerings, coming to church, working in the ministry or sharing your faith, then you can change. You can cause a desire to be born in your heart which propels you up the path of God's will to obey the Word from your heart.

Out of the Pit

One of the most undervalued and under-utilized ways to follow God's will involves the desires of your heart. We find this truth articulated in the following familiar passage from the book of Psalms:

> **Trust in the Lord, and do good; dwell in the land, and feed on His faithfulness. Delight yourself also in the Lord, and He shall give you the desires of your heart. Commit your way to the Lord, trust also in Him, and He shall bring it to pass.**

> **Psalm 37:3-5**

The first instruction the psalmist gives is to **trust in the Lord and do good.** I believe the word *trust* in the Old Testament is a synonym for the word *faith* in the New Testament. The foundation of trust, or faith, must be laid. Once you make the irreversible decision to trust God, then provision will be made for your life.

Next, the psalmist says to **delight yourself also in the Lord.** You must not stop with faith. You have to add delight to your faith because this is how the Lord begins to shape the desire, which motivates behavior.

Then you take the final step: **Commit your way to the Lord, trust also in Him, and He shall bring it to pass.** You cannot commit your way fully to the Lord until you have taken care of the desire issue. You have to lead with your heart.

Faith is the foundation. Then we delight ourselves in the Lord, and He begins to change our desires. Then our way can be committed to Him, and He will bring to pass the desires He has given us.

Handball Lesson

When I was in the Air Force, our squadron got into handball in a big way. Everyone always wanted to play handball. I did not have much of a desire to play; it made my hand swell up, and besides, I always ended up losing.

But a couple of the guys kept bothering me about it and I was tired of losing, so I worked hard enough to finally win a game. That felt so good that I started thinking about handball. I started thinking about strategy. I started getting in a little better shape. I started thinking about whipping the guy who had been beating me for two months. I started thinking about how good it felt to win.

Suddenly, I was the person organizing all the games in the squadron because I had the desire for handball.

Where did that passion come from? It developed as I started giving my thoughts and attention to the game. It was nothing I had any desire for at all until I chose to think about it. Those thoughts changed my heart.

To experience God's highest and best, you must live out of your heart. If your heart is not interested in the right things, if it is not aligned with the Word of God, you can change that by changing your thoughts.

That's what delighting yourself in the Lord is all about it.

God tells us to think about certain things.

Finally, brethren, whatever things are true, whatever things are noble, whatever things are just, whatever things are pure, whatever things are lovely, whatever things are of good report, if there is any virtue and if there is anything praiseworthy—meditate on these things.

Philippians 4:8

As we saw in Psalms, thinking about the right things generates the kind of desire which will take us in the right direction. Think about being healed instead of thinking about being sick, prosperous instead of poor, a lover instead of a hater. Think about what God has spoken to your heart—the visions He has given you, what you can be in Christ and the promises He has made to you.

93

But What If...?

A lot of people do not, or will not, do this. Instead, they say, "I do not want to get my hopes up; I might be disappointed." That is from the pit of hell. God is the author of hope.

When God shows you something, think about it, meditate on it, picture it being a reality in your life and thank Him for it. Doing this increases your desire, and the more intense your desire, the more securely you will hang on to the promise when circumstances are contrary.

Do not think about the things the world says that are contrary to the Word of God. Do not think about the doctor's report. I know what they say is real in this temporal realm, but you can choose what you think about and, therefore, what you receive.

You may not know *how* your desire rises, but you do not need to know. As you think on the things of God and as the desire for His will in your life grows, the door for God to fulfill that desire will open every single time.

We have the tendency to say, "God I have been waiting for a week and a half. Where is it?"

It will happen in due season—not a day late, nor a dollar short.

Now, you can either do it God's way, or you can do it the world's way. You can either do things from your heart, or you can be like the church at Sardis and do things because you feel guilty, condemned, obligated or coerced by tradition and empty ritual.

Being an Overcomer

When the desire comes, you can commit your way to the Lord. Now you are in a position to be an overcomer.

"He who overcomes shall be clothed in white garments, and I will not blot out his name from the Book of Life; but I will confess his name before My Father and before His

**angels. He who has an ear, let him hear what the Spirit says
to the churches."**

Revelation 3:5,6

What is to be overcome here? We are to overcome the pressure of
tradition to do things that are not in our hearts.

White garments are an analogy for the glory and presence of God.
Adam and Eve did not know they had no clothes on until fellowship with
God was broken. Then the shame of their nakedness became apparent to
them. Why? It was because they had been clothed with the presence and
the glory of God until that point.

That is the reward for living out of your heart. The people I know who
walk the closest with the Lord are the ones who live out of their hearts. If
you overcome the tendency to do things just for traditional reasons, your
reward will be the presence and glory of God every day of your life. That
makes life worth living.

CHAPTER NINE

The Lukewarm Church

Because Sardis (the church we just examined) was very wealthy, it had been repeatedly sacked by a succession of emperors and tyrants. The city had been rebuilt to a point where it was a wealthy city once again, but their wealth was mainly "old money," and Sardis was becoming decadent. They were not what they used to be, but they didn't know it.

Laodicea, in contrast, was not "old money" but was the up-and-coming, wealthy city of the day in Asia. Well-fortified and situated on the Lycus River at the center of commercial trade routes, it was probably the wealthiest of the seven cities on a per-capita basis.

The city was founded by Antiochus and was named after his wife. It had several notable characteristics. Splendid temples and theaters dotted the city, and its medical school was both excellent and well-known. But the heartbeat of Laodicea was banking and finance.

Laodicea was, we might say, a yuppie town.

Three additional facts complete the picture of Laodicea. First, it was renowned for Cerryrium, an eye salve made there exclusively. Second, near the city were several mineral streams which the people frequently visited. Third, a specialized wool industry, which produced a very high-grade glossy black wool, had developed in the city.

As we shall see, Jesus knew exactly whom He was addressing in the letter to the Laodicean church.

> **"And to the angel of the church of the Laodiceans write, 'These things says the Amen, the Faithful and True Witness, the Beginning of the creation of God: I know your works, that you are neither cold nor hot. I could wish you were cold or hot. So then, because you are lukewarm, and neither cold nor hot, I will vomit you out of My mouth.**
>
> **'Because you say, I am rich, have become wealthy, and have need of nothing—and do not know that you are wretched, miserable, poor, blind, and naked—I counsel you to buy from Me gold refined in the fire, that you may be rich; and white garments, that you may be clothed, that the shame of your nakedness may not be revealed; and anoint your eyes with eye salve, that you may see.**
>
> **'As many as I love, I rebuke and chasten. Therefore be zealous and repent. Behold, I stand at the door and knock. If anyone hears My voice and opens the door, I will come in to him and dine with him, and he with Me.**
>
> **'To him who overcomes I will grant to sit with Me on My throne, as I also overcame and sat down with My Father on His throne. He who has an ear, let him hear what the Spirit says to the churches.'"**

Revelation 3:14-22

The subject of Jesus' instruction concerns being lukewarm rather than zealous and on fire for God. The Lord was saying to the church at Laodicea, and to us today, "Lukewarm is not acceptable. Not only is it not acceptable, it is sickening to Me." That is what **"I will vomit you out of My mouth"** means. It is nauseating to God when someone is lukewarm.

I used to wonder, *Why in the world would Jesus say He would wish someone be cold rather than lukewarm? At least lukewarm is on the way to being hot. It is a little bit there.*

Then it dawned on me: People who are cold at least know they need to get by the fire; they know they need to change. They may be a long way from God, but they know they need to take some action. However, people who are lukewarm believe they are all right. They do not feel any compulsion to change. They do not know they need to get closer to the fire.

The believer who is lukewarm also has the capacity to negatively influence other marginal Christians; whereas somebody who is cold probably does not. Even a new Christian knows better than to take counsel from someone who is cold and serving the devil instead of serving God. But a lukewarm Christian has been around awhile and can look and act as though he or she has it all together.

The believers in Laodicea understood very well the point Jesus was trying to make. The nearby mineral streams would run at various temperatures. If they were hot, soaking in them could be helpful. If they were cold, then their mineral content would be healthful to drink. But if they were lukewarm, they would literally make you sick to your stomach and make you want to throw up.

Be Zealous

Then Jesus said, "Be zealous and repent." *Zeal* is defined as "enthusiastic devotion to a cause, an ideal, or a goal, and tireless diligence in its furtherance; intense or fervent desire."[1]

Being lukewarm, then, is having no zeal or intense desire. So the subject matter of this instruction is how to add the element of intensity to your desire to do your works. These folks obviously had some desire and did some works. Jesus makes reference to their works, saying they are neither hot nor cold; in other words, their works are good for nothing.

You will never influence anyone with your opinion until you become fervent—until you have an intense, white-hot desire to see it happen. This is why being lukewarm is not to be allowed. If you do not burn with passion and intense desire to see things change, then nothing will. You will just get more stagnant as your life progresses.

You have to be passionate. You have to burn with an inner intensity, which the Bible tells you how to cultivate. You must learn how to stop the forces and influences which rob you of your zeal.

Verse 17 says the Laodicean church believed they had **need of nothing.** That was the root of their being lukewarm. Here is a key point. Zeal, desire and passion are rooted in a revelation of *need.*

If you do not realize you need something, you certainly are not going to desire it. Your desire begins to form as you begin to understand your need for something. Most of the time the need for something is readily apparent. If you are sick or in a hospital, you do not need a prophecy or a word from God to know you are sick. If you cannot pay your bills, you do not need a supernatural revelation to know you need more money.

Some areas of need are much more apparent than others, and you can see clearly that they generate great desire. The greater the need, the greater the desire.

Desire and the intensity of that desire are directly related to the immediacy and relevancy of the need you have. The stronger the revealed need, the stronger the desire. In the natural, when the need is eliminated or met, there is no foundation for that desire to continue, and it wanes.

Therein lies the danger of the blessing of God.

Even though it is the will of God for us to prosper, be healthy and whole, have good relationships and be successful, as soon as the need begins to be met, we have a tendency to let our desire for the full fruition of His will begin to falter. We quit depending on God and then wonder why we are not experiencing the fulfillment of all His promises. We settle for "good enough" instead of God's best—lukewarm instead of hot.

What is the lesson to learn from the church at Laodicea? The key is in Jesus' words:

"Because you say, I am rich, have become wealthy, and have need of nothing—and do not know that you are wretched, miserable, poor, blind, and naked."

Revelation 3:17

Increase in the temporal realm has the power to blind us to our need for God. You can find this pattern repeated throughout the Bible; it is not unique to Revelation.

The increase which is the will of God for your life must be treated properly. You cannot become dependent on it or trust in the increase itself. Otherwise you will become blind to your further need for God just as the Laodiceans did. And just like that church, you will be robbed of the fire of God in your life.

What do you do to keep this from happening? Desire must be rooted in the revelation of need; and when you delight yourself in the Lord, He plants the right desires in your heart. (Psalm 37:4.)

Then when you begin to delight yourself in Him, you begin to get a revelation of what you need to complete His purpose for your life.

But when most people realize their need, they do not allow it to become the foundation of desire; and so it does not move them in the direction God wants.

How do we enhance the revelation of need in our lives? First, we do not let the revelation of need produce covetousness or discontent.

A few years ago, I bought a new fishing boat. I loved that boat. But before I had even fully learned how to run it, the Lord told me to give it away. I argued with Him for about a month. Then, after it broke down two or three times, I figured I had better give it away so it would work right.

You must view everything you have or receive as a resource for God to use. He will give blessings to you to enjoy if you do not get hung up on them. The church at Laodicea got hung up on the material increase which had been a result of the Word of God working in their life, and it blinded them to their continuing need for God and robbed them of their zeal.

Our strategy, then, is to reverse the process by understanding the danger inherent in that increase and never letting ourselves become dependent on it. We have to be ready to clean out our bank accounts at the drop of a hat (the Holy Spirit's "hat"—no one else's).

If He tells you to clean out your bank account or give away your boat or your car, can you do that? How about this one: **"Sell whatever you have and give to the poor"** (Mark 10:21)?

If you cannot, you are in the same situation as that rich young ruler, and you will not inherit eternal life any more than he did.

> **Jesus said to him, "If you want to be perfect, go, sell what you have and give to the poor, and you will have treasure in heaven; and come, follow Me."**
>
> **But when the young man heard that saying, he went away sorrowful, for he had great possessions.**
>
> **Matthew 19:21,22**

The Solution

So what is the solution to this pseudo-sophistication, studied complacency and lack of fervency? What did the Laodicean need? What does our American church need?

> **"I counsel you to buy from Me gold refined in the fire, that you may be rich; and white garments, that you may be clothed, that the shame of your nakedness may not be revealed; and anoint your eyes with eye salve, that you may see."**
>
> **Revelation 3:18**

Sounds a bit odd, doesn't it? The solution is gold refined in the fire, white garments and eye salve?

Yes. The church in Laodicea knew exactly what Jesus was talking about. The believers in this city of high finance and big-money deals were told to buy **gold refined in the fire;** they were to return to works of pure and honest value.

The city famous for sleek black wool was told to buy fine white garments typical of the linen used by the priests. And the city famous for its eye salve was told it needed a spiritual eye salve for its own blindness.

Gold Refined in the Fire

In other words, return to something which is pure and has true value; go back to the solid foundation of Jesus Christ. Fancy theologies just create a lukewarm attitude, but the true and pure foundation of faith in the finished work of Jesus will allow you to rekindle the fire of your life in God. Then you can build on that foundation with the building materials called good works.

Now if anyone builds on this foundation with gold, silver, precious stones, wood, hay, straw, each one's work will become clear; for the Day will declare it, because it will be revealed by fire; and the fire will test each one's work, of what sort it is.

If anyone's work which he has built on it endures, he will receive a reward. If anyone's work is burned, he will suffer loss; but he himself will be saved, yet so as through fire.

1 Corinthians 3:12-15

This refers to the judgment seat of Christ, which is for giving out rewards for work done. All the things we have done in this life are either going to be wood, hay and stubble—garbage to be burned up by the fire of God—or they will be in the category of gold, silver, precious stones—good works that will survive the trial of fire.

You cannot be lukewarm and do works which are this enduring gold. The remedy for being lukewarm is to live out of your heart. Do not do something just for the sake of doing it. Base your life on the Word which you have put into your heart. Build your trust in His Word by meditating on it day and night.

For example, if the Holy Spirit has spoken to you to have a new building downtown, then you need to think about it day and night. You may not know how you are going to get it. You may not know the steps you have to take, but you do not need to. Meditate on it day and night, and the Lord will order your steps.

> **The steps of a good man are ordered by the Lord, and He delights in his way.**
>
> **Psalm 37:23**

There is one last element we have to consider in this section: Jesus said, **"Buy from Me gold refined in the fire,"** the enduring gold (Rev. 3:18). That means there is a cost attached to it. If you want to deal a death blow to the lukewarmth in your life, it will cost you something.

There are two ways this applies to us. One is in a specific sense, as it relates to material things. The other is in a general sense, as it relates to this temporal realm we live in.

White Garments

Laodicea had enough money to be comfortable and to feel as if they did not need God or anything else. Therefore, if they were going to do from their hearts things that were consistent with the Word, it was going to cost them their dependence on money or material wealth.

The believers in the city that produced the highest quality worldly garments of glossy black wool were counseled by Jesus to buy from Him the more lightweight, less protective, less impressive white garments typically worn by priests, whose first responsibility was to serve the Lord. Their identity was not to be vested in what they wore, but in whom they served.

One of the costs of doing the will of God is your dependence on money and material possessions. You cannot be dependent on them anymore. Our trust is to be in the Lord, if we are going to serve Him.

> **Command those who are rich in this present age not to be haughty, nor to trust in uncertain riches but in the living God, who gives us richly all things to enjoy.**
>
> **1 Timothy 6:17**

This means that in order to do God's will you are going to have to plant some seed—give some things away. That is exactly why Jesus told the rich young ruler what He did. If you are going to break your dependence on money, you are going to have to start giving it away as the Lord directs.

Eye Salve

The believers in the city that produced the world-renowned Cerryrium eye salve were counseled by Jesus to anoint their eyes with spiritual eye salve to heal their blindness.

What blindness? The church at Laodicea had measured their level of need only by natural considerations and blinded themselves to the spiritual truth they needed to see. God could not reveal any further need to them. They blinded themselves by leaning on temporal, natural considerations. No wonder Jesus told them they needed eye salve.

In order to live consistently out of your heart, it will cost you the ability to see things from a natural viewpoint only. You simply cannot lean on the natural, temporal realm anymore. Learn to place your trust in the leading of the Holy Spirit. You may feel as though you are being lead around like a blind person for a while, but Jesus' salve will do its job. Soon you will see the world and your situation as He does.

For example, a certain businessman had $50,000 to use, and in the natural, his business logic told him to invest it into his business. As a matter of fact, he knew he might have cash-flow problems if he did not. But his heart's desire was to plant the money into a ministry, so he did. It cost him dearly not to let his natural, logical, rational approach to business dictate how he would use the money. Jesus' salve had done its work, and he was now able to see his situation from Jesus' viewpoint.

For our light affliction, which is but for a moment, is working for us a far more exceeding and eternal weight of glory, while we do not look at the things which are seen, but at the things which are not seen. For the things which

**are seen are temporary, but the things which are not seen
are eternal.**

2 Corinthians 4:17,18

The Greek word translated *look* in this verse does not mean "to visually gaze at." It means "to give consideration, focus, or attention."[2] In other words, do not give your attention to, or focus with your physical eyes on, the natural realm—what you can see.

Now, God is not telling you to take your brain and lay it aside. Your natural ability to calculate and deduce is important. It is God-given. But He is saying those things have to be secondary to the unseen realm. That is where your focus has to be. Learn to depend more on the leading of the Holy Spirit than on what you can see and deduce.

We know about the unseen realm, the realm of the spirit, the heavenly realm and the eternal truths which cannot be touched, tasted or felt. These truths are revealed to us by the Word of God and the word spoken to our hearts through the Holy Spirit. This is how that realm is discerned:

But as it is written: "Eye has not seen, nor ear heard, nor have entered into the heart of man the things which God has prepared for those who love Him." *But God has revealed them to us through His Spirit.* **For the Spirit searches all things, yes, the deep things of God.**

1 Corinthians 2:9,10

Do you know what you need in order to realize your divinely appointed destiny? The phrase **"Eye has not seen, nor ear heard, nor have entered into the heart of man"** means you cannot find those things for yourself.

You cannot get enough education, experience or insight to figure it out for yourself. Those things are only revealed "through His Spirit" while you are "on the job."

The things which are seen are *temporal.* That means they're temporary, or subject to change. But the things which are not seen are eternal. Hang your hat on the eternal words of God. Make them what you look at and focus on; then the need will be made clear, and your obstacle will be insignificant and momentary.

The Reward

Now, the reason for buying from Jesus gold refined in the fire is **"that you may be rich"** (Rev. 3:18). You might think, *But the Laodiceans were already rich!* No. They had money, but they were not rich. There is a big difference. You can have money and still be like them—wretched, miserable, poor, blind, naked and too dumb to know it.

> **The blessing of the Lord makes one rich, and He adds no sorrow with it.**
>
> **Proverbs 10:22**

Your real wealth is stored in heaven and is put there by your good works that are motivated by your heart, not just by a feeling that you "should."

Secondly, the benefit of buying from Jesus **"white garments"** is **"that you may be clothed, that the shame of your nakedness may not be revealed."**

White garments are always symbolic of the glory of God, the presence of God in a person's life. If you live out of your heart, His presence will clothe you, and His glory will be wherever you are. Your identification will be with Him, and you can proudly say of Jesus, "Whose I am, and whom I serve."

And lastly, the benefit of anointing **"your eyes with eye salve"** is **"that you may see."** What was the Laodicean church's problem? They could not see their need, because they only looked at themselves from the natural perspective. Revealed need is the basis of all fervency, desire or zeal. They could not *see*, and they were *lukewarm* as a result.

Excited About Living

The bottom line is that if you will take Jesus' counsel, you will be zealous, on fire and passionate. Life will take on new meaning. Every day you will get out of bed excited about living. And in this condition, you will be highly effective for God. Lukewarmth will not be a part of your life.

CHAPTER TEN

The Word Church

So far we have examined six of the seven churches:

Ephesus, the "works church."

Smyrna, the "persecuted church."

Pergamos, the "deceived church."

Thyatira, the "worldly church."

Sardis, the "traditional church."

Laodicea, the "lukewarm church."

Now we are going to look at the seventh and last church, the church at Philadelphia, "the Word church."

Philadelphia was second to last in the string of churches Paul founded in that area. It was located midway between Sardis and Laodicea and was just a little east of them. The city was a center of Greek culture when it was built around 200 B.C.; but by the time of the writing of this letter, it had a very large Jewish population.

Philadelphia was famous for its wine making and survived until A.D. 17, when it was destroyed by an earthquake. Tiberius Caesar saw this catastrophe as a door of opportunity to expand the influence of Rome, and he rebuilt the city shortly thereafter.

Here, then, is Jesus' letter to this most favored of churches, which had just lived through times of great change. How tempting it must have been to flow with the tides of change rather than remain true to God's Word.

"And to the angel of the church in Philadelphia write, 'These things says He who is holy, He who is true, "He who has the key of David, He who opens and no one shuts, and shuts and no one opens": I know your works. See, I have set before you an open door, and no one can shut it; for you have a little strength, have kept My word, and have not denied My name. Indeed I will make those of the synagogue of Satan, who say they are Jews and are not, but lie— indeed I will make them come and worship before your feet, and to know that I have loved you. Because you have kept My command to persevere, I also will keep you from the hour of trial which shall come upon the whole world, to test those who dwell on the earth.

'Behold, I am coming quickly! Hold fast what you have, that no one may take your crown. He who overcomes, I will make him a pillar in the temple of My God, and he shall go out no more. And I will write on him the name of My God and the name of the city of My God, the New Jerusalem, which comes down out of heaven from My God. And I will write on him My new name. He who has an ear, let him hear what the Spirit says to the churches.'"

Revelation 3:7-13

The church at Philadelphia is the only church of the seven which received neither correction nor instruction. Five of the churches received correction; the church at Smyrna did not receive correction, but they did receive instruction about how to handle the pressure which comes from contrary circumstances.

But the Philadelphian church did things so well that Jesus did not say anything to them other than, "Keep doing what you are doing."

What did they do? Very simple: They kept the Word. That was all they did. Verse 8 says they **"have kept My word, and have not denied My name,"** and verse 10 says, **"You have kept My command to persevere."**

You must understand that *keeping the Word* means "consistently *doing the Word.*"

Many believers will say, "Yes, I believe the Word," but they do not do it. Doing what the Word says is a convenience, rather than a matter of lifestyle, for them. They go to church when it is convenient and when they do not oversleep. They pray when it is convenient and when they have the time. They give their tithes when the financial pressure is not too great, and they give some offerings when they have a little extra.

Jesus said in Luke 6:48-49 that if you do not want the storms of this life to blow your house down, then you must build on a firm foundation and not on the sand. He said that foundation comes from doing the Word you hear.

Faith comes by hearing, but it is not enough to hear the Word and believe. To keep the house of your life from being blown down, you must act on what you have heard. James 2:17 says, **Thus also faith by itself, if it does not have works, is dead.**

The bottom line is being a doer of the Word, and that is what the church at Philadelphia was. They did the Word consistently, not just when it was convenient; it had become their lifestyle. They were constantly persevering in the pursuit of making the Word of God alive and active in their lives. And their reward for doing so was significant.

The Reward, Part 1

The first part of their reward was in Revelation 3:8:

**"I know your works. See, I have set before you an open
door, and no one can shut it; for you have a little strength,
have kept My word, and have not denied My name."**

The "open door" Jesus refers to is an opportunity, which no man can stop
or take away from them, to step into His will.

If you do the Word of God, there will be doors of opportunity for you to
step through in your life as well. No one will be able to shut those doors—
not your spouse, your children, your coworkers or your boss.

I have people tell me, "I have a gift I want to share, but this church just
has not made a way for me to exercise my gift."

The Bible says a man's gift (not the pastor) makes room for him. God
will open doors for you to walk into the place where you are called to be if
you are a doer of the Word. Do not try to convince me that some person or
circumstance has closed the door of God's will to you.

Here is another thing I hear frequently: "I believe I should be doing this
or that, but because a person in a position over me does not like me, it hasn't
happened." The "it" could be a raise, a promotion or a ministry opportunity.

The truth is that the problem is sitting in your seat right now. I say this in
love, but the problem is *you*. I would not want to offend anybody, but I want
you to have an opportunity to deal with the truth and quit running from it.

Here is that truth: If you want the will of God for your life, you have just
one simple thing to do—*be consistently obedient to do the Word of God.*

We are not talking about church tradition or the doctrines of men; we
are talking about reading the Word for yourself, cleaning out your spiritual
house of any junk you used to believe and basing your life on the Word.

The evidence of your success will be open doors that no man can
shut. This is the first reward of being a doer of the Word.

The Reward, Part 2

**"Indeed I will make those of the synagogue of Satan,
who say they are Jews and are not, but lie—indeed I will**

make them come and worship before your feet, and to know that I have loved you."

Revelation 3:9

No longer will the kingdom of darkness dominate you. No longer will you be under the heel of somebody who is serving the devil or his purposes. You will dominate the forces of darkness—everything and every demon in it.

These truths will make you want to do the Word. They will keep you from putting the blame somewhere else. No man can shut these doors. No force of darkness can dominate you. Quit saying, "Satan did this to me." You have no reason for darkness to dominate your life. You cannot change something until you accept the responsibility for it. That is where the reward begins.

The Reward, Part 3

The third reward is perhaps the best. Verse 10 says, **"Because you have kept My command to persevere, I also will keep you from the hour of trial which shall come upon the whole world, to test those who dwell on the earth."**

That means you will go in the Rapture of the church if you are a doer of the Word. The only believers who are promised the Rapture are those who consistently base their lives on the Word of God and are doers of the Word.

People say, "God is no respecter of persons. If you are a member of the church, you are going to go in the Rapture." That is simply inconsistent with Scripture. We can see from the parable of the ten virgins in Matthew 25 that this is just not the case. (vv. 1-13.)

There is only one class of Christian who is going, and that is the Christian who does the Word consistently, lives by faith and bears the fruit of righteousness as a result.

I am not talking about a specific church or denomination. There are Christians in every church—Catholic, Baptist, Lutheran, Methodist and so forth—who keep the Word and do it consistently from their hearts.

Those who are doing so are the ones—the only ones—who Jesus has guaranteed will miss the "hour of trial" on this earth. This is a truth we have to embrace. The Rapture is real. It is not something you can spiritualize by saying, "Well, it is not a literal catching away."

That is unbiblical, traditional junk. Many persuasions of Christianity teach that the Rapture is not literal or real. Those folks are going to be here during the hour of trial. They will not participate in something they have no faith for. You partook of salvation by faith, got baptized in the Holy Spirit by faith, and you will or will not participate in the Rapture of the church by faith.

First Thessalonians 5:9 says that we are not appointed to wrath. Therefore, if we will consistently pursue being doers of the Word, we will not be here to experience God's wrath.

No one can live a perfect life on his or her own. That is not what we are talking about here. We are talking about walking according to the leading of the Holy Spirit (Rom. 8:4), who enables us to live according to the Word.

Only those who live in the Spirit will understand what lies beyond, hear the voice and the trump and go in the Rapture of the church.

It is a simple truth that you cannot fully live in something you do not fully have—or only have in limited measure. You have to be filled with the Spirit if you are going to live there.

If you are not baptized in the Holy Spirit with the evidence of speaking in other tongues or if you do not know what it means to be filled with the Spirit, you have to come to grips with your need to open your heart to this experience.

Paul made it clear that there is an experience subsequent to salvation called the baptism in the Holy Spirit. On several occasions in the book of Acts, Paul asked new believers if they had been filled with the Holy Spirit since they had believed.

When you are saved, you become a temple of the Holy Spirit; but then you need to fill the temple. That is the next step—the baptism in the Holy Spirit.

Yielding to that indwelling presence is how you remain filled. It is not just a matter of getting baptized one time or speaking in tongues once to meet the requirements.

When you speak in tongues, it is the evidence of being filled initially. So when you speak in tongues and pray in the Spirit, you are acknowledging His indwelling presence; and it stirs Him up in you. The Word says, **He who speaks in a tongue edifies himself** [or builds himself up] (1 Cor. 14:4). That is why we pray in the Spirit.

Pray in the Spirit all throughout the day, at home, in the shower, under your breath while at work. When you do, you are saying to the Holy Spirit, "I believe You are in there, and I want you to fill me to the limit with revelation— the things I need to know to succeed in life, the things You want me to do and the things which illuminate Your plan for my life."

He will fill you with this illumination. That is His job.

But What If I Sin?

First John 1:9 says, **If we confess our sins, He is faithful and just to forgive us our sins and to cleanse us from all unrighteousness.** That is part of the Word too. However, the fact that we can obtain forgiveness does not eliminate the call to consistency.

Consistency is still a requirement for blessing. We cannot say, "We can go out and party on Friday night and then repent on Sunday morning." We cannot say, "I can sleep with my girlfriend one more time and then repent the next day."

Romans 6:15 says, **Shall we sin because we are not under law but under grace? Certainly not!** When we make mistakes, we can restore our fellowship with God, but that does not mean we have suddenly elimi- nated the need to be consistent.

On the contrary, we return to "Go," do not collect $200 and have to start over again.

The Rapture of the Church

Immediately following the letters to the seven churches, John's account recorded in the book of Revelation takes a remarkable turn.

After these things I looked, and behold, a door standing open in heaven. And the first voice which I heard was like a trumpet speaking with me, saying, "Come up here, and I will show you things which must take place after this."

Immediately I was in the Spirit; and behold, a throne set in heaven, and One sat on the throne.

Revelation 4:1,2

John finds himself in the presence of God "immediately"—in the blink of an eye. John's experience is a foreshadowing of the Rapture of the church. Just look at the similarities to this passage about the Rapture in 1 Corinthians 15:51-53:

Behold, I tell you a mystery: We shall not all sleep, but we shall all be changed—in a moment, in the twinkling of an eye, at the last trumpet. For the trumpet will sound, and the dead will be raised incorruptible, and we shall be changed. For this corruptible must put on incorruption, and this mortal must put on immortality.

There are many religions which teach the immortality of the spirit, but Christianity is the only one which teaches the eventual immortality of the body. It is one of the tenets which make us unique among all other religions.

At the Rapture, the dead will be raised first and will put on incorruption (receive their glorified bodies), and then we who are alive and remain will be changed in the twinkling of an eye.

But I do not want you to be ignorant, brethren, concerning those who have fallen asleep, lest you sorrow as others who have no hope. For if we believe that Jesus died and rose again, even so God will bring with Him those who sleep in Jesus.

For this we say to you by the word of the Lord, that we who are alive and remain until the coming of the Lord will by no means precede those who are asleep. For the Lord Himself will descend from heaven with a shout, with the voice of an archangel, and with the trumpet of God. And

the dead in Christ will rise first. Then we who are alive and remain shall be caught up together with them in the clouds to meet the Lord in the air. And thus we shall always be with the Lord.

1 Thessalonians 4:13-17

If you believe that Jesus died and rose again, then you have to embrace the Rapture of the church. Just as the death and the Resurrection of Christ are fundamental and intrinsic to our beliefs, the Rapture is as well. It is clearly part of our biblical doctrine as Christians.

CHAPTER ELEVEN

The Judgment Seat

For we must all appear before the judgment seat of Christ, that each one may receive the things done in the body, according to what he has done, whether good or bad.

2 Corinthians 5:10

The first stop for you in your new body will be before the judgment seat of Christ. The Lord is going to present to Himself a glorious body, without spot or wrinkle or blemish. (Eph. 5:27.)

How will that be accomplished? Ephesians 5:26 says Jesus **will sanctify and cleanse** [the church] **with the washing of water by the word.** Can we, because of the washing of water by the Word, come to a place where we have no blemishes? No, that is only how the process begins. We cannot walk perfectly before God until that Day; nobody can reach a state of perfection in this earth. So all the blemishes which are not removed on this earth through the Word, He will remove in heaven before we are presented to Him as His bride, the church.

The physical imperfections will go when we receive our glorified bodies, but the works we have done in our earthly bodies still have to be accounted for before we become a glorious church.

The wood, hay and stubble—the things we do in these bodies which are blemishes—are going to be burned up. Only the good will remain. Only then can we be presented to Jesus as His glorious bride.

The purpose of the judgment seat of Christ is to finish the purification process. You got rid of your old heart when you were born again, you get rid of your old body at the Rapture of the church and Jesus gets rid of your blemished works at the judgment seat of Christ.

> **According to the grace of God which was given to me, as a wise master builder I have laid the foundation, and another builds on it. But let each one take heed how he builds on it. For no other foundation can anyone lay than that which is laid, which is Jesus Christ.**
>
> **1 Corinthians 3:10,11**

The building of your life is your responsibility, not God's. He changes you supernaturally when you make Jesus your Lord. Then the foundation is laid, but what you build on that foundation is up to you.

> **Now if anyone builds on this foundation with gold, silver, precious stones, wood, hay, straw, each one's work will become clear; for the Day will declare it, because it will be revealed by fire; and the fire will test each one's work, of what sort it is.**
>
> **1 Corinthians 3:12,13**

The Day Paul is speaking of is the day on which we will go before the judgment seat of Christ:

> **If anyone's work which he has built on it endures, he will receive a reward.**
>
> **1 Corinthians 3:14**

The judgment seat is for the purpose of distributing reward, not punishment. **If anyone's work is burned, he will suffer loss....** Loss of what?

Loss of his reward. **...but he himself will be saved, yet so as through fire** (1 Cor. 3:15).

The judgment seat of Christ does not have anything to do with your salvation. Rather, it has to do with your works done on this earth. The wood, hay and stubble will be burned up. The gold, silver and precious stones will remain; and for those, you will receive a reward.

The Basic Challenge

So this is our basic challenge: Once the foundation of Jesus is laid, we must begin building with gold, silver, precious stones—things which are going to survive the trial of fire.

What constitutes the gold, silver and precious stones? What makes something wood, hay and stubble? To survive the trial of fire, your works have to be in line with the Word of God—both the written Word and the word the Spirit speaks to your heart. Those kinds of works also have to come from your heart. These are the works for which you will receive a reward.

What kind of rewards is Jesus talking about? In Matthew 25, we have the parable of the talents: A lord goes on a far journey and entrusts his belongings to his three servants. To one he gives five talents, to another two and to another one. Then after a period of time, he returns and an account must be made.

After His resurrection, Jesus ascended to the right hand of the Father. Upon the church He conferred dominion, authority and His name to bring increase to the kingdom of God. And just as surely as the returning lord in the parable took an account of what he had entrusted to his stewards, so will our Lord take an account when He returns.

The Account

The first two servants in the parable brought increase to their lord, and he said to them, **"Well done, good and faithful servant; you were**

faithful over a few things, I will make you ruler over many things. Enter into the joy of your lord" (v. 21).

When your works on this earth produce an increase for the kingdom of God in the earth, the reward will be an eternal one—ruling and reigning with Jesus for an eternity.

The extent of that eternal rulership and the exact shape and nature of it will depend upon what you do in this life.

It costs you something eternal in nature when you live for the world instead of God. You must become mindful of the things you do on this earth, because they are setting the stage for your experience in eternity.

Rewards are also fulfilled desires. The desires which are fulfilled on this earth are rewards from God for being faithful to do the Word.

But we all will probably have some desires which are not yet fulfilled when He calls us up. I'm convinced that God will shape our eternal destinies in a way that enables us to fulfill those desires.

The Third Servant

There was, however, a third servant involved, and things did not go so well for him. He buried his lord's investment, and as a result he was not given the same response as were the other two:

> **"Therefore take the talent from him, and give it to him who has ten talents.**
>
> **"And cast the unprofitable servant into the outer darkness. There will be weeping and gnashing of teeth."**
>
> **Matthew 25:28,30**

That punishment always seemed pretty tough to me. I had a problem with this for a while because Scripture says all three were servants of the lord and were entrusted with his resources. And just because one was unprofitable, he was cast out into "outer darkness"; he was sent to hell.

I used to think, *That sounds as if you must earn your salvation by works.* Yet we know **by grace you have been saved through faith, and that**

not of yourselves; it is the gift of God, not of works, lest anyone should boast (Eph. 2:8,9).

This parable seems to teach that if we, as the Lord's servants, do not work hard enough to be profitable, we are going to hell. My confusion evaporated, however, when I discovered that "outer darkness" in this verse is not a reference to hell. The root of the Greek word translated *outer* here simply means "away."[1] And the word *darkness* does not mean "complete elimination of light." It means "shadiness";[2] there is still *some* light, but it is neither direct nor bright.

The following passage from 1 Corinthians brings some illumination to this issue:

> **There is one glory of the sun, another glory of the moon, and another glory of the stars; for one star differs from another star in glory. So also is the resurrection of the dead.**
>
> **1 Corinthians 15:41,42**

To put it plainly, your works don't determine whether or not you make it to heaven, but they do determine how close to the glory you'll be when you get there.

Some people are going to be right there standing in front of the Lord with the light of His glory shining as brightly as the sun on them. Others will be in less glory, as in moonlight; others still less, as in starlight.

There are some servants whose works are completely unprofitable, who will be far away in the shadows. The word "unprofitable" means your spiritual balance sheet is comprised almost entirely of wood, hay and stubble rather than gold, silver and precious stones.

That is what will cause the weeping and gnashing of teeth. Think how painful it would be to stand before the judgment seat of Christ and watch everything you did in this life burn up. It would be even more painful to realize you wasted your life. It will be a grievous experience for some.

Understand, this grief is not punishment being meted out by God. This is going to be our response to standing before God and realizing we wasted a lifetime on this earth chasing after worthless things that the world said were important.

John's Advice

And now, little children, abide in Him, that when He appears, we may have confidence and not be ashamed before Him at His coming.

1 John 2:28

This verse leaves little room for doubt. There are going to be some in the church who will be "ashamed" at the Lord's coming. The only way to avoid that shame is to **abide in Him.** This is the same as living in the Spirit and basing your life on the Word, doing your works from your heart.

Shame is defined in the dictionary as "great sorrow or sadness, by virtue of disgrace."[3] The Word associates it with "weeping and gnashing of teeth."

Now, we know that in heaven as we live out our eternal destiny there is no weeping or tears, so this feeling of shame is a momentary thing as we stand before the judgment seat.

But I want you to see there is a downside to the judgment seat for the people who suddenly realize they have done nothing for God. The sudden, awful realization that they have lived according to a wrong standard will bring great shame and an overwhelming sense of disgrace—and thus weeping and gnashing of teeth.

But if you will base your life on the Word of God, you will stand before His judgment seat to hear Him say, "Well done, good and faithful servant. You have been faithful over a few things; I am going to make you ruler over much. Enter into the joy of your Lord."

You are going to be launched into eternity with a joy and excitement we cannot even begin to imagine right now.

CHAPTER 12 TWELVE

The Fear of the Lord,
PART 1

Revelation 4 begins with a type of the Rapture; then the balance of the chapter is a description of the grandeur, the magnificence and the glory of God. This same indescribable sight is the first thing we will see upon our arrival in the heavenly realm.

We will be affected the same way as the twenty-four elders: We will be on our faces before His throne, overcome by a sense of holy awe and reverence at the mighty presence of God.

The apostle John had the impossible task of trying to communicate the overwhelming magnificence of God with mere human words.

> **Immediately I was in the Spirit; and behold, a throne set in heaven, and One sat on the throne. And He who sat there was like a jasper and a sardius stone in appearance; and there was a rainbow around the throne, in appearance like an emerald.**
>
> **Revelation 4:2,3**

The apostle John compares God's appearance to the beauty of precious stones. Jasper is a transparent, light green gem similar to jade, and sardius is a semi-transparent stone with bands of red, like an agate.

Around the throne were twenty-four thrones, and on the thrones I saw twenty-four elders sitting, clothed in white robes; and they had crowns of gold on their heads.

Revelation 4:4

Some scholars suggest these are redeemed men; others contend they are angels. To me, it is clear the former is the more accurate interpretation—they are redeemed men.

It is reasonable to assume the twenty-four represent the heads of the twelve tribes of Israel and the twelve apostles.

The Lord said Abraham's descendants would be as numerous as the sand on the seashore, referring to the natural seed of Abraham—the children of Israel, which consist of twelve tribes, each tribe having a head, or elder. The Lord also said Abraham's descendants would be as numerous as the stars of heaven, referring to Abraham's spiritual seed—the body of Christ, with the twelve apostles representing the elders of that branch.

And from the throne proceeded lightnings, thunderings, and voices. Seven lamps of fire were burning before the throne, which are the seven Spirits of God.

Revelation 4:5

Here we have a reference to the presence of the Holy Spirit around the throne. Isaiah 11:2 makes it clear there is a sevenfold anointing of the Holy Spirit, and this is referred to here as **the seven Spirits of God.**

Before the throne there was a sea of glass, like crystal. And in the midst of the throne, and around the throne, were four living creatures full of eyes in front and in back. The first living creature was like a lion, the second living creature like a calf, the third living creature had a face like a man, and the fourth living creature was like a flying eagle. And the four living creatures, each having six wings, were full of eyes around and within. And they do not rest

day or night, saying: "Holy, holy, holy, Lord God Almighty, Who was and is and is to come!"

Revelation 4:6-8

I think about these beasts and am reminded of how little we really know about the realm we will inhabit for eternity. There are all kinds of creatures populating this universe.

And yet God says you are the apex of His creation. You have been created to rule and reign with Him. That means you have a universal assignment, which might mean you will be a representative of almighty God in some outpost of the universe to bring His Word, His light and His Spirit to bear.

Contrary to common belief, you are not going into eternal retirement when you go home to be with the Lord. You are just beginning.

These many-eyed creatures in chapter 4 seem to have a guardian role of some sort around the throne; they also lead the worship in the heavenly realm.

Whenever the living creatures give glory and honor and thanks to Him who sits on the throne, who lives forever and ever, the twenty-four elders fall down before Him who sits on the throne and worship Him who lives forever and ever, and cast their crowns before the throne, saying: "You are worthy, O Lord, to receive glory and honor and power; for You created all things, and by Your will they exist and were created."

Revelation 4:9-11

I think the importance of this chapter is not in who the beasts or the twenty-four elders are or what all the symbolism is. The significance of this chapter is that our arrival in heaven is accompanied by an immediate immersion into the glory, the holiness, the grandeur of God.

This says to me that without a holy awe, a reverential awe—something the Word often refers to as the "fear of the Lord"—we will not be equipped for our eternal destiny, nor for our millennial destiny.

Reverential awe, or the fear of the Lord, causes you to go to your knees when you experience His presence. When you consider deliberately doing something counter to the Word, your heart immediately rejects it because of your reverence for the Spirit, the Word and the person of God. Reverential awe and fear keep you on track as nothing else will.

The church today is permeated with casual lethargy toward God in our lives. We rely on the grace of God to cover our continuing errant ways. That behavior demonstrates an absence of the fear of the Lord.

The most fundamental consideration of all is the fear of the Lord. It is more basic than faith, love or any other Bible principle. Without it, nothing else will happen for you. Our lives have to become grounded in the fear of the Lord.

Certainly, I realize God's nature and character have many facets—He is our Redeemer, our lover, our forgiver, the One who extends grace and mercy, our loving heavenly Father—and many people need to see these sides of Him. But we do not spend enough time on the side of God which brings judgment to the earth.

The revelation of that side of God is the foundation of the fear of the Lord. I believe it is the most foundational concern of all, and yet it is one which is conspicuously absent from contemporary churches. There would not be any yawning or sleeping in church if the people had a reverential awe of God.

When you have a genuine fear of the Lord, you will not have to be dragged to church, and you will not grumble and gripe about the tithe, put off your prayer time because you need a little extra sleep or do that dirty deed you were considering.

If that reverential awe is a reality to you, it will forever alter the way you live.

The Principal Thing

As if that weren't enough, there is another reason to make sure you have cultivated a healthy fear of the Lord in your life. It has to do with the value of *wisdom*.

Wisdom is the principal thing; therefore get wisdom. And in all your getting, get understanding.

Proverbs 4:7

128

Wisdom is the principal thing—not faith or love or prayer. What is wisdom? I have heard *wisdom* defined as the ability to put knowledge to work and have it produce the desired result. It begins with knowledge, certainly; but it cannot stop there. If knowledge does not produce the desired result, you are in need of wisdom.

We all know a few "knowledgeable idiots." They have reams of knowledge and can quote facts from morning till night, but their lives are in shambles. They have not been able to make knowledge work for them. They do not have wisdom; they are not wise.

The most important knowledge we can have is the Word of God. This is the truth we build our lives upon. But just to know what God has provided for you without experiencing it is not good enough. You can know about healing, but if you cannot attain it in your body, you need wisdom. Why? Because wisdom is the ability to make knowledge produce fruit.

We should constantly be in the pursuit of wisdom because it is the principal thing. It is founded on the Word of God, so you have to read the Word and hear the Word. That brings faith, which does not work without love. All of the other principles come into play in wisdom. The ability to put the Word to work in your life is what wisdom is all about.

Putting It Together

The fear of the Lord is the beginning of wisdom, and the knowledge of the Holy One is understanding.

Proverbs 9:10

Wisdom is the principal thing, and the *beginning* of wisdom is the fear of the Lord. You will never get serious enough about the Word to make it produce if your life is not founded in the fear of the Lord.

The word *fear,* as used in the Bible, has two possible meanings. One is reverential awe; the other is anxiety, or concern you will experience harm in one form or another. We know God has not given us a spirit of fear; that comes from the devil. We have no reason to fear that God would do us harm.

So **the fear of the Lord** is a reverential awe of God due to His magnificence and holiness. This awe would keep you from ever intentionally doing anything to be a reproach, disappointment, embarrassment or mockery to Him. It is a *profound* respect for the things of God.

More Benefits

The secret of the Lord is with those who fear Him, and He will show them His covenant.

Psalm 25:14

The **secret of the Lord** to me is the mysteries talked about in the New Testament related to our covenant with God. Much of your personal destiny, God's plan for your life, His covenant with you regarding the call on your life, is secret. It is not recorded in the Bible; it must be revealed by the Holy Spirit.

We see that these secrets are only going to be revealed to those who fear Him.

You say, "I wish I knew what the Lord had for my life. I wish I knew what I am supposed to do now." I would suggest the problem could be inadequate reverence for the things of God and the fear of the Lord operating in your life.

If He destined you to be a millionaire businessman, do you think He will trust you with those millions if you are not grounded in a reverential fear of the Lord? You would use it for yourself; nothing would restrain you from abusing the resources He would provide.

No, those things are going to remain a secret, a mystery, until you consecrate your life to Him in the fear of the Lord.

Another wonderful benefit of cultivating a healthy reverence for God is that it results in a lack of "want." Take a look:

Oh, fear the Lord, you His saints! There is no want to those who fear Him.

Psalm 34:9

We all have wants. To see them satisfied, we must become more reverent about our lives in God. **There is no want to those who fear Him** means wrong desires as well: You will not want any more alcohol, drugs, cigarettes or wrong relationships. And your right desires will be fulfilled. That is what it means to have no wants.

> **Wisdom and knowledge will be the stability of your times, and the strength of salvation; the fear of the Lord is His treasure.**
>
> **Isaiah 33:6**

The NIV translation of verse 6 tells us this *treasure* is "salvation and wisdom and knowledge." The fear of the Lord is the key to that treasure.

Salvation includes more than just your eternal destiny in heaven. It includes healing, preservation, protection and provision. Until we evict selfishness out of our hearts and make room for the reverential awe of the Lord, there will not be room for the greater blessings.

Response to Redemption

> **And if you call on the Father, who without partiality judges according to each one's work, conduct yourselves throughout the time of your stay here in fear; knowing that you were not redeemed with corruptible things, like silver or gold...but with the precious blood of Christ.**
>
> **1 Peter 1:17-19**

To be able to *do* the Word on a consistent basis in this life and to stand before the judgment seat of Christ with works of gold, silver and precious stones, you must spend your time on earth in the fear of the Lord.

Whether it has to do with wisdom or the meeting of wants or needs in our lives, experiencing the presence of God or being able to live our lives righteously before God on a consistent basis, the foundation of it all is the fear of the Lord.

Here is what is at stake: miracles, signs and wonders, the harvest, blessings, revival and the outpouring and manifestation of the glory and presence of God.

First Chronicles 13 records an Old Testament example of the price for failing to fear the Lord. When David brought back the ark of the covenant from captivity, it was placed on a cart pulled by oxen. When the oxen stumbled, the ark began to slip off, and a man named Uzza put his hand up to stop it from toppling. When he did, he was struck dead.

David could not understand it; they were just trying to bring the presence of God back to Jerusalem where it belonged.

In so many words, God said to David, "You did not reverence My Word enough to have the priests carry it on their shoulders as I instructed. You were careless about your approach to My presence."

They did not revere God's word as priority when in His presence, and it cost Uzza his life.

In Acts 5, Ananias and Sapphira experienced the same thing. A lot of faith people ask, "Why did our loving God kill these people just because they did not give everything they had acquired from the sale of their land?"

The Day of Pentecost launched a glorious revival and mighty move of the Holy Spirit, and there was a manifest presence which produced a great release of finances. People sold their goods and pooled everything to promote the gospel. The church was under great persecution at this time, but no one withheld anything. The highlight was Barnabas, a wealthy man from Cyprus, who sold his land and gave all of the proceeds to the apostles.

Ananias and Sapphira were wealthy people who had always supported the church. Now, seeing this Cypriot newcomer named Barnabas sell his property and give *all* the money to the gospel, Ananias and Sapphira felt their status discounted. So they sold their property, too, but the sale generated more money than they were willing to give to the gospel.

So they said, in effect, "This is too much money to give to the church, so we will hold part of it back. But we want everybody to think we are giving it all, just as Barnabas did. So we'll just give a portion and say it was all the money we got for the sale of our property."

Peter did not ask them, "Why did you keep some?" He asked, "Why did you lie to the Holy Ghost?" If they had truly had a revelation of God's greatness and holiness, do you think they would have lied to Him to impress people?

This was not about the money; this was about their irreverence and absence of the fear of the Lord. They could not withstand the glory of God with that attitude, and they died.

One detail about this incident that most people overlook is the fact that a great spiritual awakening resulted:

> **So great fear came upon all the church and upon all who heard these things. And through the hands of the apostles many signs and wonders were done among the people. And they were all with one accord in Solomon's Porch.**

> **And believers were increasingly added to the Lord, multitudes of both men and women, so that they brought the sick out into the streets and laid them on beds and couches, that at least the shadow of Peter passing by might fall on some of them. Also a multitude gathered from the surrounding cities to Jerusalem, bringing sick people and those who were tormented by unclean spirits, and they were all healed.**

> **Acts 5:11,12;14-16**

Do you want to be part of the coming great harvest of souls? Do you want signs, wonders, miracles and the flow of the supernatural in your life? These all follow the fear of the Lord.

Notice that when great fear and great reverence came upon them, a flow of power was released which forever changed the face of the earth.

It is not God's will that any man should perish. But He is a righteous judge, and when He manifests His presence among human flesh, the fear of the Lord allows us to experience His glory and power without suffering an adverse affect.

The Lord, in His mercy, has withheld the strong outpourings many of us have prayed for, because we could not survive them if He released them. The fear of the Lord is an absolute necessity if we as the church are going to experience the fullness of what God wants.

CHAPTER THIRTEEN

The Fear of the Lord,
PART 2

I f you understand the importance of the fear of the Lord, the next thing you will want to know is *how* you develop that awesome reverence in your life.

There are two principle patterns in the Bible which relate to the development of the fear of the Lord in someone's life. We see the first pattern in Leviticus:

> **And Moses and Aaron went into the tabernacle of meeting, and came out and blessed the people. Then the glory of the Lord appeared to all the people, and fire came out from before the Lord and consumed the burnt offering and the fat on the altar. When all the people saw it, they shouted and fell on their faces.**
>
> **Leviticus 9:23,24**

The first pattern is when the presence of the Lord is manifest and the people respond. Leviticus chronicles a response which can only be described as reverential awe. The people fell on their faces. All of them, that is, except two; and they happened to be priests, the sons of Aaron.

> **Then Nadab and Abihu, the sons of Aaron, each took his censer and put fire in it, put incense on it, and offered profane fire before the Lord, which He had not commanded them. So fire went out from the Lord and devoured them, and they died before the Lord.**
>
> **Leviticus 10:1,2**

The word *profane* means "contempt or irreverence for what is sacred."[1] Why were the actions of Aaron's sons irreverent? They took unwarranted liberty by putting their own incense fire in censers which were intended for the worship of the Lord and then offering it before the Lord.

Not only that, but they had not been directed to offer incense in the first place. They did something not commanded by God, and they did it in a profane manner. They took irreverent liberty to do it their way.

One of them may have said, "We are all out of that other kind of incense; we will just use this instead." All of the others were on their faces revering the presence of God, and they decided to do something "priestly," something religious. They ignored the manifest presence of God, choosing instead to bring attention to themselves, and it cost them their lives.

> **And Moses said to Aaron, "This is what the Lord spoke, saying: 'By those who come near Me I must be regarded as holy; and before all the people I must be glorified.'" So Aaron held his peace.**
>
> **Leviticus 10:3**

Think about that for a moment. Aaron, who had just lost his two sons, **held his peace.** He feared the Lord.

The Lesson To Be Learned

Just because we are temples of the Holy Spirit and have been redeemed by the blood of Jesus does not mean we are excused from the principles of the Word. If the manifest glory of God comes and there is irreverence in His presence, judgment is the result.

Now, we do not like to hear a lot about judgment. We would much rather hear about prosperity, healing, running in the aisles, joy and laughter. But there is a side of God which is righteous and holy, and He is the Judge of all the earth. Judgment is a fact of our relationship with God.

It is not God's intent to bring His hammer of judgment down in retribution, but this is the picture many people have painted of God over the years. They have seen bad things happening to people as God bringing His fist of judgment down in retribution on those who have angered Him. Much of the *King James Version* of the Bible is rendered that way because the translators did not know any better.

But as we understand the loving, caring side of God, who does not wish that any should perish, we can understand that judgment has different sides. There are different types of judgment.

One form of judgment is already in the earth today. Because of Adam's sin, the world operates under a curse. Essentially, it is the removal of God's intimate, manifest presence. Wars, famines, pestilence, murders and more are all the result of this curse working in the earth.

There are many who say in their ignorance, "If there were a God, or if God cared about us, this world would not be such a mess." Wrong! If there were not such a large number of people who irreverently denied and mocked the very existence of God and took it upon themselves to live their lives their own way, *then* this world would not be such a mess.

Living Free From the Curse

There is a curse operating in the earth; and in the Old Testament, God's provision for deliverance from that curse was obedience. **"And all these blessings shall come upon you and overtake you, because you obey the voice of the Lord your God"** (Deut. 28:2). So they could live the blessed life instead of the cursed life, but only through obedience to God.

The problem in the Old Testament was that unregenerate man had no capacity to obey with consistency, so they experienced the curse periodically.

But in the New Testament, Jesus has been made a curse for us. (Gal. 3:13.) Therefore, once we have been cleansed by the atoning blood of Jesus, when we make a mistake and confess it before God, we are restored to fellowship with Him and cleansed from all unrighteousness. (1 John 1:9.)

But here is the point I want to make: *Deliberate disobedience still puts you under the curse today.* If you consistently disobey, you are going to be touched by the curse. If that is your lifestyle—if there are things in your life you know must change, but you get up every morning and confess the same sin over and over and over—you are irreverent. You have no fear of the Lord, and you are exposed to the judgment of the curse already operating in the earth.

Another Judgment

There is another judgment we see in the story of Aaron's sons: If God manifests His glory while you are in a grossly irreverent state, you are going to be judged. My intent in telling you this is not to frighten you but you have to know the truth.

It is not God's will that any should perish, but He is not going to withhold His presence or glory from this earth indefinitely. He is going to wait for as many people as possible to get right with Him before He comes.

If He were to manifest Himself in all His glory to us right now, most of us would not survive it.

We complain about not seeing more of God than we see. Why are there not more miracles and healings? Why is there not a greater measure of God's presence in evidence?

I think a large part of the reason is that we do not have a holy fear—a deep down, consuming reverence for God, which would enable us to survive that manifestation. And He does not want us to die. He is waiting for us to develop a fear of the Lord so He can manifest His glory and His presence to us. Then, instead of bringing judgment, He could bring us blessing.

When you are properly connected to God in fellowship with Him and He manifests Himself to you, healing, provision and blessings come.

So this is the first pattern: There is a manifestation of God's glory; judgment comes; the fear of the Lord is the result, and obedience follows.

Aaron feared the Lord after judgment came upon his sons. And I guarantee you, he got it right the next time. No priests offered censers with profane fire ever again, and the people enjoyed the manifest presence of God and the blessings of His presence.

Remember Uzza? The man who tried to steady the ark of the covenant on the way back into Jerusalem and was struck dead by God? King David was confused and angry at first, but then a great fear came on him. The Word says, **David was afraid of God that day, saying, "How can I bring the ark of God to me?"** (1 Chron. 13:12).

Just like Aaron, after the judgment came and the fear of the Lord was established, David did not make the same mistake again:

> **David built houses for himself in the City of David; and he prepared a place for the ark of God, and pitched a tent for it. Then David said, "No one may carry the ark of God but the Levites, for the Lord has chosen them to carry the ark of God and to minister before Him forever." And David gathered all Israel together at Jerusalem, to bring up the ark of the Lord to its place, which he had prepared for it.**
>
> **He said to them, "You are the heads of the fathers' houses of the Levites; sanctify yourselves, you and your brethren, that you may bring up the ark of the Lord God of Israel to the place I have prepared for it. For because you did not do it the first time, the Lord our God broke out against us, because we did not consult Him about the proper order."**
>
> **So the priests and the Levites sanctified themselves to bring up the ark of the Lord God of Israel.**
>
> **1 Chronicles 15:1-3, 12-14**

They had that word the first time, but they ignored it. That is irreverence, and you cannot dance, sing or praise enough to cover up irreverence. David learned this the hard way. Once he did it right, Israel brought the ark of God back to Jerusalem where it belonged, and the people were greatly blessed.

Ananias and Sapphira were struck dead because of their irreverence in the manifest presence and glory of God. (Acts 5.) Great fear of the Lord and reverence followed, and then the miracles, the blessings, the power and the signs and wonders came, and many were saved.

This pattern is all throughout the Word. When the presence of God manifests, He is either going to bring blessing or judgment, depending on the condition of your heart and your reverence for God.

You can just imagine what the people were thinking who knew Ananias and Sapphira: *That could have happened to me. I could have done that. If it had been me, I could be dead now.*

Imagine if this happened to someone you know really well, someone you respect. Would that not drive you to your knees in a way you have never known before? It is that kind of reverence which releases signs, wonders, healings, miracles and the harvest in the church.

Where there is irreverence, there will be judgment. Where there is a reverential awe of God, the fear of the Lord, there will be blessing. And where judgment comes, it will produce reverence in those who remain. When God gets a group of people who fear the Lord as they should, great things can happen.

The Second Pattern of Judgment

The second pattern takes place if the proper reverence and the fear of the Lord are already established when God manifests His presence and glory.

Prior to His ascension, Jesus told the disciples to go to Jerusalem and wait to receive power. Five hundred people were present when the waiting began, but only 120 received a visitation from the Holy Spirit. Why? Only those few did because the rest of them did not reverence the Lord or His word to them.

Some of them probably hung around a couple of days after He ascended and then said, "Well, He is gone now. We might as well get back to our lives. We cannot wait forever." Others might have said, "He said we should go to the uttermost parts of the earth, right? No point in waiting; we should get busy doing something."

But there were 120 of them who said, "I do not care if I *rot* in this upper room, I am going to wait on the promise of the Spirit *because that is what Jesus told me to do!*"

They had the fear of the Lord, and that made it impossible for them to disobey what He said. Only the 120 who remained were baptized in the Holy Spirit that day.

Because of their reverence, the whole world was shaken. Peter came out and preached a message, and 3000 people were saved. **Then fear came upon every soul, and many wonders and signs were done through the apostles** (Acts 2:43).

There does not have to be judgment to produce the fear of the Lord. Peter, filled with the Holy Spirit and power, preached an anointed sermon, speaking to people in their own languages, and there were supernatural signs and wonders. There was a manifestation of God's presence and glory, but no judgment came upon them, because they already had the fear of the Lord.

So the second pattern *begins* with the fear of the Lord, which produces glory and blessing. This is the pattern we must learn to live in. We must become reverential people, who operate in the fear of the Lord *before* we see the manifestations which will bring judgment to the irreverent.

There is a way to do that. There is a way to open yourself to the Holy Spirit so He can bring you a fresh revelation of God's grandeur, magnificence and holiness. There is a way you can operate in the fear of the Lord, bringing in the glory, instead of being judged by it, and moving in great blessing.

We are going to follow one of two patterns. We will either come to fear the Lord because of the judgment which falls on the irreverent, or we will come to fear the Lord on our own. Then He will release His glory, and the blessing will follow.

These two patterns are all throughout the Word. When the presence of God manifests, it is either going to bring blessing or judgment. Look in your heart and you will know which it would be for you—blessing or judgment.

If you need to make some changes, take comfort in knowing that change is only a choice away.

CHAPTER FOURTEEN

The Fear of the Lord,
PART 3

The fear of the Lord is not something which just happens, nor is it something you can work up. You cannot say, "I think I will be reverent now." *This kind of reverence comes by a revelation of the Holy Spirit to your heart.* The Holy Spirit has to reveal God's majesty and holiness to you, or you will never experience it.

When He does give you that revelation, it drives you to your knees, and you cannot help but be dumbstruck in your spirit by the wonder of the Lord. Then the fear of the Lord will rise in you speedily.

If it does not happen, you are not going to realize the blessing, the anointing or the power of God in your life on a consistent basis. It is, therefore, crucial that we diligently seek this revelation.

To begin doing so, we must be honest with ourselves. We cannot say, "I have not murdered or slept around or stolen. I am not doing too badly; I am all right." The "little" sins are no better than the "big" ones. Sin is sin, and it all removes us from fellowship with God.

These six things the Lord hates, yes, seven are an abomination to Him: a proud look, a lying tongue, hands that shed innocent blood, a heart that devises wicked plans, feet that are swift in running to evil, a false witness who speaks lies, and one who sows discord among brethren.

Proverbs 6:16-19

This refers to being proud or haughty, telling little white lies, exaggerating, stretching the truth, having evil thoughts toward those whom you dislike or who have wronged you, deciding to sin when you know better because you can "confess and repent tomorrow" and being critical and judgmental of fellow Christians.

Most of these things do not fit our category of "major" sin, but they are an abomination to God. We have to face the fact that we cannot be casual about the Word of God, calling ourselves reverent or saying we operate in the fear of the Lord, when there are secret, unaddressed sins about which the Lord has spoken to us.

Cultivating the Fear of the Lord

The fear of the Lord is cultivated by seeking God. Seeking the Lord is the way we allow the Holy Spirit to reveal to us God's wonder and greatness and holiness and bring the fear of the Lord to bear in our lives.

I am convinced most Christians do not know how to seek God. They have such a religious view of what it means to be seekers of the Lord.

The religious style says, "You have to close yourself up in your prayer closet for days at a time or fast until you pass out or repent in sack cloth and ashes. You have to deny yourself of anything in this natural realm you even vaguely want and do extreme things to seek the Lord." The implication is that God is hiding and has to be coaxed into a relationship.

This view of seeking the Lord either pushes people completely away or locks those who are hungry for God into a works program, keeping them constantly under condemnation. It is not biblical.

There is an order, a way to begin seeking the Lord, which is proper and in line with the Word.

Get Your Priorities Right

"But seek first the kingdom of God and His righteousness, and all these things shall be added to you."

Matthew 6:33

This Scripture does not say, "Seek second or third or fourth." Nor does it say, "Seek first your business, your educational pursuits or the things you are saving for."

The word *kingdom* is defined as "a realm or domain where a single entity is dominant; the rulership of a sovereign."[1] The kingdom of God is a universal kingdom because He is the Creator of this universe. But more than that, He is the source of life in this universe. Spiritual laws and principles govern His kingdom, and the Word is the revealer of them to us.

What you are actually doing when you **"seek first the kingdom of God"** is seeking, first and foremost, to base your life on the Word of God, on the revelation of His kingdom for your life.

The Consecration of Submission

Because the rulership of His kingdom is by a sovereign God, we must submit ourselves to His purpose, to His plan, to His will. Implicit in the mandate to seek first the kingdom of God is our understanding of the need to be consecrated to the will of God.

To be a seeker of God, you must be consecrated to the pursuit of His will. Let me put it this way: If you are interested in getting into the presence, the glory and the person of God, then the *will* of God is the highway that will take you there.

The farther down that highway you go, the more of His presence you will experience. Ultimately, the will of God will take you up in the Rapture, right into the throne room and then on into an eternity of rulership with Him.

In this earthly life, the best way to reach the person of God is to understand and pursue the will of God, as revealed by the Word and by the Spirit to our hearts. It does not just happen to you. Because He made you a free moral agent, you have to make choices which align your life with His will.

That is why seeking first the kingdom of God and consecrating your life to His will have to be your *first* priorities.

Locating the Kingdom

Next, you must know where the kingdom of God is located.

In Luke 17:21, Jesus said, **"The kingdom of God is within you."** You do not have to look into the heavens to find the kingdom of God.

John 3:3 tells us how the kingdom gets there. **"Most assuredly, I say to you, unless one is born again, he cannot see the kingdom of God."**

Why do you think there is so much controversy over the term "born again"? The enemy knows he has to keep the kingdom of God out of as many people as he can because when they receive it, they become a threat to him. Once you are saved and the kingdom of God is born in your spirit, you have access to the will of God and to the divinely appointed destiny He has for you.

Relating to the King and His Kingdom

"Assuredly, I say to you, whoever does not receive the kingdom of God as a little child will by no means enter it."

Mark 10:15

We cannot lay hold of the kingdom of God unless we come with the innocence of children. This kingdom within you, with all of its dreams and aspirations, has to be received with the same kind of innocence, excitement and absolute trust that a little child has.

But as it is written: "Eye has not seen, nor ear heard, nor have entered into the heart of man the things which God has prepared for those who love Him."

1 Corinthians 2:9

God has prepared some things for you and for me which no one has ever seen, heard or thought before. You cannot take enough aptitude tests, go to enough colleges or talk to enough wise men to discover what you ought to do with your life. Only God can teach you; and He will because He wants you to be a world changer, an overcomer. He wants you at the top of the ladder, not the bottom. He has prepared marvelous things.

But God has revealed them to us through His Spirit. For the Spirit searches all things, yes, the deep things of God.

1 Corinthians 2:10

This is why the Holy Spirit was given. His ministry in this dispensation is to reveal and then empower you to pursue the plan of God. His ministry is revelation.

The Role of Prayer

For what man knows the things of a man except the spirit of the man which is in him? Even so no one knows the things of God except the Spirit of God. Now we have received, not the spirit of the world, but the Spirit who is from God, that we might know the things that have been freely given to us by God. These things we also speak, not in words which man's wisdom teaches but which the Holy Spirit teaches, comparing spiritual things with spiritual.

1 Corinthians 2:11-13

Prayer is a lot of what seeking God is about. As you begin to pray in the Spirit, some of it will be in your understanding, some of it will be in tongues— **not in words which man's wisdom teaches but which the Holy Spirit teaches.** Even when the words are not fruitful to your natural understanding, interpretation can come to you; so be sure to ask for it.

Do not be irreverent and mock God's Word when it says you need to be filled with the Holy Spirit. Some pastors say, "We do not want to alienate any of our carnal, secular visitors, so we will leave that tongues stuff out of our sermons. We will teach folks they received all of the Holy Spirit they are going to get when they were born again; tongues died with the New Testament church." Then they wonder why they do not see any more of God in the lives of their flock.

Go to the Word. If you reverence God, you reverence the Word. The Word says Jesus is the One who baptizes in the Holy Spirit and fire. (Luke 3:16.) It also says that Jesus is the same yesterday and today and forevermore. (Heb. 13:8.) If Jesus is always the same, He can still baptize you in the Holy Spirit.

The baptism in the Holy Spirit opens you to the fullness of the Spirit in your life.

He is there, in your spirit, to reveal the things God has prepared for you which no eye, ear or mind has experienced yet. He will begin to open to you the will of God for your life. Your divinely appointed destiny then begins to become clear.

As you pray in the Spirit, you will have dreams and visions; you will find things in your heart which begin to excite you and stir you up. You will sense things happening in your heart which could never happen without yielding to the indwelling presence of the Spirit of God.

This is why praying in the Spirit is so important. This kind of prayer accesses the ministry of the Holy Spirit and puts you in the flow of God's will for you.

Pizza Fantasies or Holy Ghost?

Now, when these things begin to be revealed to you, they will change your view of life. But they can also seem like fantasies you'd normally attribute to too much pizza the night before. So be careful what you do with the revelations given to you.

If then you were raised with Christ, seek those things which are above, where Christ is, sitting at the right hand

of God. Set your mind on things above, not on things on the earth.

Colossians 3:1,2

When the Holy Ghost begins to show you things in prayer and these dreams, ideas and desires begin to be born in your heart, do not write them off and never think about them again. Write them down and start putting your mind on them. Start building a vision of your future from what God has shown you by the Spirit. Think about them. This is why the Bible says to meditate day and night on the Word of the Lord.

Cultivate Your Heart

The Word of God is a seed, and the heart of man is the soil. (Mark 4.) If you will consistently, regularly and methodically steep yourself in the Word of God—read it, hear it, say it, memorize it and meditate on it—you will develop more faith for the things the Holy Spirit has revealed to you. The soil of your heart will soften and accept the seed of the Word, which will germinate, take root and produce fruit.

Guarding Against Thorns

Once there has been fruit produced, you have to guard against thorns, weeds and bad seeds which grow up to choke out the Word. They come in three principle forms: **the cares of this world, the deceitfulness of riches, and the desires for other things** (Mark 4:19).

The cares of this world are fear or anxiety. You start sweating something. When you do not have anything, you do not really worry; but once you have things, you start getting a little anxious about losing them.

As the Word begins producing fruit, you can become anxious about it. "I wonder if this is really going to keep on working." Cares and anxieties can become a part of your life. Worry will choke the Word.

The deceitfulness of riches refers to the greatest challenge of all— prosperity. It is not the will of God for you to become dependent on money

149

instead of Him. The challenge of prosperity is remaining detached and independent of your material possessions. Staying in the Word will help you see possessions as resources to use however God wills. But once you become dependent on your income or your material wealth to address the needs you perceive in your life, you have fallen into the trap of the deceitfulness of riches.

> **Command those who are rich in this present age not to be haughty, nor to trust in uncertain riches but in the living God, who gives us richly all things to enjoy.**
>
> 1 Timothy 6:17

Deceitfulness of riches is fundamentally fear—fear of loss—and we have not been given a spirit of fear. Fear chokes faith right out of your spirit.

The desires for other things refers to covetousness. We all have a tendency to pursue self-gratification in one form or another; but the closer we draw to God, the more outwardly directed our concerns will become. The folks who think only of themselves or think of themselves first are going to have a very hard time operating in faith. This will choke the Word out of their lives.

If you avoid these three types of thorns—worldly cares, dependence on possessions and covetousness—then you become good, fertile soil and Satan is not able to steal the Word. If you stand and do not get offended when affliction or persecution comes; if you continue weeding the garden of your heart, keeping the fears and anxieties out and remaining independent of reliance on money or material possessions; if you keep the motives of your heart oriented toward others, then you are in position for God to make maximum use of you. If you do all that, you will produce a thirty-, sixty- or hundredfold return on the Word sown in your heart.

Summary

Live out of your heart. Be true to your heart, because that is where the greater One lives, where He plants the desires which guide your every step, where the will of God for your life is revealed and where your joy, strength and excitement are born.

Your heart is where the seed has to be sown to produce an increase in your life. The heart is the rallying point for how you seek God. You are seeking first the kingdom of God as you learn to identify your heart's desires.

As you become skilled in listening to your heart and begin to have faith in the dreams and visions God has revealed, you will begin to seek first His kingdom and the will of God for your life. The further down that path you walk, the more of the manifest presence of God you will experience.

As you seek first the kingdom of God in this fashion, you will be growing more reverent of the Lord on a daily basis, developing a fear of the Lord which allows His manifest presence and glory to bring the blessings, power, miracles and harvest of souls to your life. You will receive an awesome return on your investment of time to develop the fear of the Lord!

CHAPTER FIFTEEN

Seven Dispensations and Daniel's Seventieth Week

The next event, after our introduction to the presence and glory of God, is the opening of the seven seals of the scroll; no one is worthy to open them except Jesus.

The scroll and its seven seals represent the events which occur during the seven-year period of time on earth called the Tribulation.

Here is what will happen in heaven: the judgment before the seat of Christ, our presentation before the throne of God, the marriage supper of the Lamb, the preparation for our return with the Lord, the Battle of Armageddon and His Second Advent.

Now we will see what happens on earth during the same seven years. The events which occur on earth are represented by the seven seals. Loosing, or breaking open, these seals is necessary to completely open the scroll.

To understand the Tribulation, we must understand the prophecy of Daniel's Seventieth Week in Daniel 9. I have heard one teacher say end-time prophecy is like a big wheel with a lot of spokes, and the hub is Daniel's Seventieth Week. All of the spokes of prophecy begin to make sense if you have the hub in place.

It is also like the box top on a jigsaw puzzle. If you have a jigsaw puzzle with 2000 pieces and you scatter the pieces on the floor and throw away the box top with the completed picture, you will have a lot of trouble putting it together properly. The picture in Daniel helps us put the pieces of Revelation together properly.

The Seven Dispensations

God's dealing with mankind is generally viewed in terms of dispensations. A dispensation is a time period during which God relates to humankind in a particular way. There are seven human dispensations wedged between the eternal ages past and the eternal ages to come.

They begin with the "dispensation of innocence," when Adam in his innocence walked with God in the cool of the Garden. The dispensation of innocence ended with the sin and fall of man.

At that point, God dealt with humanity through the "dispensation of conscience." That continued until the time of Noah.

Then the "dispensation of civil government" began. God directed the standard of behavior for mankind through the civil law which was given to Noah. That dispensation continued until the time of Abraham.

God's dealings with Abraham began the "dispensation of promise," wherein faith became a factor in the way God dealt with mankind. This period continued up to the time of Moses, when God gave the law, the Word of God.

Then came the "dispensation of the law." This is also called the Jewish dispensation, which continued until the first coming of Jesus, His crucifixion and resurrection and the launching of the New Testament church.

But the dispensation of the law, or Jewish dispensation, did not actually end there! It was only temporarily suspended until after the next dispensation.

The "dispensation of grace," or the church age, began with the availability of salvation by grace through faith in Jesus and will continue until the Rapture of the church.

After the church is taken out of the earth, the final seven years of the Jewish dispensation, which was interrupted by the church age, will be finished. This period, also known as the Tribulation, will be the time of the greatest outpouring of God's wrath upon this earth ever experienced by humanity.

At the close of those seven years of Tribulation, the Second Advent of our Lord will occur. At that time, Christ will return as King of kings, defeat the forces of Antichrist at the battle of Armageddon and set up His earthly, millennial reign.

The Judgments

There are several judgments during these last periods. We have the judgment seat of Christ, which is for the saints in heaven and occurs after the Rapture of the church.

The judgment of the living nations will occur after Jesus has defeated the Antichrist, and its purpose will be to determine which nations of peoples will actually go into the Millennium. There will be people going into the Millennium who are not saved. There will be people in the Millennium who do not even know Jesus has come back to this earth.

During the millennial reign of Christ, Satan will be bound in chains and cast into the pit. But at the end of that 1000 years he will be released to see whom he may deceive; he'll even target God's elect.

For 1000 years, mankind will have had no deception at work in their lives. The Lord will give every person on earth one final opportunity to respond to Him while the deceiver is out of the earth. I know it is a shock, but there will be multitudes who will not respond to God's grace but will rebel.

At the conclusion of that short time when the rebellion is put down, the Great White Throne judgment will occur. All of the living and dead who are not in Christ will stand before the Great White Throne of God. This is not a believer's judgment; this is for the unbeliever. All of those who have sided with Satan and have exercised their free moral wills to serve him instead of God will be consigned to be with him eternally in the lake of fire. Satan, too, and his demonic host will stand before the Great White Throne of God for their eternal judgment and consignment to the lake of fire.

At the close of the Millennium, this earth will be purified by fire and a new earth will come into existence, free from the corruption which man's tenure in his depraved state has brought to the earth.

Everything will be renewed, and the earth will once again become a pristine garden. Then God will transfer the capital city of heaven, the New Jerusalem, to earth, where He will reside for the eternal ages to come with His creation, mankind.

The Tribulation: Daniel's Seventieth Week

With a greater understanding of God's timeline for His creation, we are now going to turn our attention to Daniel's Seventieth Week, the seven-year period of time on this earth called the Tribulation which completes the dispensation of the Jews. Here is the background.

Daniel, along with many others from Israel, was in captivity in Babylon. While there he studied the writing of Jeremiah and other Scriptures and was able to discover several important prophecies. One of these was that the captivity of the Jews would only last seventy years.

Now let us go further back and see what was behind that prophecy.

During the reign of King David, Israel loved and served God's purposes more than they had at any other time in history. But as soon as David died, Israel began to backslide as a nation. Their downward spiral continued unabated for 490 years.

It began with what seemed a very small thing. God had directed that every seventh year was to be a sabbatical year for the land; it was to lie fallow and not be used for planting that year. Six years of planting, one year of rest—that was the pattern.

But after David died, the people no longer gave the land a sabbatical rest; they began farming it year after year after year. For 490 years they disobeyed God's direct order. That amounted to seventy missed Sabbaths.

Leviticus 26 even lists some of the things the Lord said would happen, yet no one heeded this warning:

"And after all this, if you do not obey Me, but walk contrary to Me, then I also will walk contrary to you in fury; and I, even I, will chastise you seven times for your sins. You shall eat the flesh of your sons, and you shall eat the flesh of your daughters. I will destroy your high places, cut down your incense altars, and cast your carcasses on the lifeless forms of your idols; and My soul shall abhor you. I will lay your cities waste and bring your sanctuaries to desolation, and I will not smell the fragrance of your sweet aromas. I will bring the land to desolation, and your enemies who dwell in it shall be astonished at it. I will scatter you among the nations and draw out a sword after you; your land shall be desolate and your cities waste."

Leviticus 26:27-33

You could look at those verses and say, "Boy, the Lord is really being tough on these poor folks."

Remember though, He gave them 490 years to turn it around. God is long-suffering, and His mercy endures forever; but He is also a just God whose patience is limited.

The Israelites could have turned their situation around 489 times. They could have actually heard one of the prophets, repented and gotten back on the right track, and they would have missed the Babylonian captivity. But they did not.

God told them what the penalty would be for not allowing the land to rest as He commanded. They began with simple disobedience—farming the land every seventh year instead of allowing it to rest—but it became much worse than that. Their whole system became polluted.

> Moreover all the leaders of the priests and the people transgressed more and more, according to all the abominations of the nations, and defiled the house of the Lord which He had consecrated in Jerusalem.

> And the Lord God of their fathers sent warnings to them by His messengers, rising up early and sending them, because He had compassion on His people and on His dwelling place.

> But they mocked the messengers of God, despised His words, and scoffed at His prophets, until the wrath of the Lord arose against His people, till there was no remedy.

> **2 Chronicles 36:14-16**

How many times have we heard messengers of God, prophets of God, being mocked and derided by the secular society in which we live? That is a bad sign. God is merciful, but there will come a day of reckoning. That day came for the Israelites when they were defeated and led into captivity.

> Therefore He brought against them the king of the Chaldeans, who killed their young men with the sword in the house of their sanctuary, and had no compassion on young man or virgin, on the aged or the weak; He gave them all into his hand.

> And all the articles from the house of God, great and small, the treasures of the house of the Lord, and the treasures of the king and of his leaders, all these he took to Babylon. Then they burned the house of God, broke down the wall of Jerusalem, burned all its palaces with fire, and destroyed all its precious possessions.

> And those who escaped from the sword he carried away to Babylon, where they became servants to him and his sons until the rule of the kingdom of Persia, to fulfill the word of the Lord by the mouth of Jeremiah, until the land had enjoyed her Sabbaths. As long as she lay desolate she kept Sabbath, to fulfill seventy years.

> **2 Chronicles 36:17-21**

For 490 years, Israel had ignored the Sabbath for the land and seventy Sabbaths had gone unobserved. Therefore, the nation remained in captivity for seventy years so the land could remain desolate and enjoy her Sabbath rest. Daniel read these things and understood the number of the years.

Beyond Captivity

When Daniel began praying about this he also inquired of the Lord about what was to happen after the captivity was over. And as is often the case, when he asked God for something, He gave superabundantly more than he could ask or think. (Eph. 3:20.)

Not only did Daniel receive the answer to his inquiry about what was going to happen to Israel after the captivity, but the Lord continued to reveal His plans all the way up to the Second Advent of Jesus!

In Daniel 9:24-27, we have a description of what is called Daniel's Seventieth Week.

> **"Seventy weeks are determined for your people and for your holy city, to finish the transgression, to make an end of sins, to make reconciliation for iniquity, to bring in everlasting righteousness, to seal up vision and prophecy, and to anoint the Most Holy."**
>
> **Daniel 9:24**

Who are **your people?** They are the Jews; Daniel was a Jew. And what is **your holy city?** It is Jerusalem.

"Seventy weeks are determined...." The word *determined* literally means "cut off."[1] A certain period of time is cut out of God's eternal scheme of things to deal with the Jews and the holy city.

This was done to end the sin and backsliding and to bring in everlasting righteousness, the millennial reign, the anointing of the Most Holy. When will that be? It will be at the Second Advent, the return of Jesus, when He is going to be anointed the Most Holy, the King of kings and the Lord of lords. That is when righteousness will be permanently established in this earth.

The term *weeks* is misleading. I have occasionally wondered why the translators insisted on using the word "week." If you look it up in a concordance, the word simply means "sevens," in this case, "seventy sevens."[2] Since each seven years was to have been a Sabbath year, this reference is to seventy Sabbaths, not weeks.

Those seventy sevens, or Sabbaths, would equate to 490 years, which was the exact amount of time from the reign of King David and the beginning of Israel's backsliding, to the full manifestation of their apostasy and the Babylonian captivity. Therefore, God uses that same time frame to take them back up to the Millennium, to the Second Advent—seventy sevens, or Sabbaths, 490 years.

Breaking It Down

Now, the 490-year time frame is broken down in the next three verses this way: There are the first seven weeks—forty-nine years. Then there are sixty-two weeks—434 years. Then come the final seven years, the Seventieth Week, at the end of which is the Second Advent and the establishment of the earthly reign of Jesus.

The timing for all of this is revealed in the next verse:

> **"Know therefore and understand, that from the going forth of the command to restore and build Jerusalem until Messiah the Prince, there shall be seven weeks and sixty-two weeks; the street shall be built again, and the wall, even in troublesome times."**
>
> **Daniel 9:25**

The event which begins the countdown is the decree to rebuild Jerusalem, which is found in Nehemiah 2. King Artaxerxes decreed that the walls, the city and the temple must be rebuilt. That started the 490-year clock's ticking.

This is not just in the Bible. It is a part of secular history as well.

The first seven "sevens" was to be the rebuilding process for the temple and, sure enough, the history books and the books of Ezra and Nehemiah confirm that it took exactly forty-nine years from the time of Artaxerxes' decree to the completion of the rebuilding of the temple—seven weeks, seven sevens, forty-nine years. That is the first seven-year division.

The second division is the 434 years, or sixty-two "sevens," after the rebuilding of the temple. Here is what was to happen then.

> **"And after the sixty-two weeks Messiah shall be cut off, but not for Himself; and the people of the prince who is to come shall destroy the city and the sanctuary. The end of it shall be with a flood, and till the end of the war desolations are determined."**
>
> **Daniel 9:26**

What does "**Messiah shall be cut off, but not for Himself**" mean? It means He will be "cut off" for you and for me. By the stripes of Jesus we are healed; the chastisement of our peace was on Him. (Isa. 53:5.)

This 434-year division ends in A.D. 29, the year Jesus was crucified. Then we see in the balance of verse 26, **"The people of the prince who is to come shall destroy the city and the sanctuary. The end of it shall be with a flood, and till the end of the war desolations are determined."** This is a different prince than in verse 25, where Daniel talks about Messiah the Prince. This is after Messiah is cut off, and it is the prince who is to come.

Some people believe this is a reference to Satan, because he is called the prince of the power of the air in the New Testament. But this is a literal person, the same person who is referred to in verse 27. As you will see later in our study, this clearly is a reference to the Antichrist, "**the prince who is to come.**"

It is the Antichrist's people who will destroy the city and the temple again. In Revelation we see the Antichrist raised up out of the old Roman Empire.

"Why couldn't Daniel just say 'Romans'?" you ask. No one knew who the Romans were back when this prophecy was given to Daniel. There were no such people.

After sixty-two weeks, "**Messiah shall be cut off**"—that was the crucifixion—by **"the people of the prince who is to come"**—those were the Romans. In A.D. 70 the Roman emperor Titus destroyed Jerusalem, burned the temple and dispersed the Jews across the face of the earth, where they have been for most of the 2000-year period of the church age.

The one week which has not yet happened we see in the next verse.

> **"Then he shall confirm a covenant with many for one week; but in the middle of the week He shall bring an end to sacrifice and offering. And on the wing of abominations shall be one who makes desolate, even until the consummation, which is determined, is poured out on the desolate."**
>
> **Daniel 9:27**

The "he" in this verse is the Antichrist. The **"covenant with many"** is not the covenant we have with God. No, it is another covenant. It is a "covenant of peace," which we will be reading about later.

The Last Week–Daniel's Seventieth Week

So the last week has not happened yet. The first sixty-nine weeks have occurred, and the church age is wedged between the sixty-ninth and seventieth weeks. We are still in the church age. The last week, or the last seven years of the Jewish dispensation, is Daniel's Seventieth Week.

You might say, "How can you just stick 2000 years in between the sixty-ninth and seventieth weeks? What gives you the right to do that? If there is really a church age in there between week sixty-nine and week seventy, do you not think Daniel would have seen it? Why did God not show that to Daniel?"

No Old Testament prophet saw the church age. Daniel, Isaiah, Jeremiah, Ezekiel, Zechariah—none of them saw the church age.

One of the most well-known verses at Christmas time is Isaiah 9:6:

> **For unto us a Child is born, unto us a Son is given; and the government will be upon His shoulder. And His name will be called Wonderful, Counselor, Mighty God, Everlasting Father, Prince of Peace.**

But Isaiah never saw the church age. The government is not going to be upon Jesus' shoulder until His millennial reign is established. His first coming, the First Advent, is described in the first part of the verse: **Unto us a Child is born, unto us a Son is given.** Isaiah missed an entire dispensation between that phrase and **the government will be upon His shoulder.**

Jesus Quotes Isaiah–Partly

When Jesus stood up in the synagogue in Nazareth and read from Isaiah 61, proclaiming Himself as Messiah, He did something very interesting. Here is what Jesus said.

> **"The Spirit of the Lord is upon Me, because He has anointed Me to preach the gospel to the poor; He has sent Me to heal the brokenhearted, to proclaim liberty to the captives and recovery of sight to the blind, to set at liberty those who are oppressed; to proclaim the acceptable year of the Lord."**
>
> **Luke 4:18,19**

But Jesus did not finish the passage he was reading. When He had read all He wanted to, He handed the scroll back and said, **"Today this Scripture is fulfilled in your hearing"** (Luke 4:21).

In other words, only part of the passage in Isaiah was fulfilled. The rest was for later. What was the rest? Here is the part of the passage Jesus did not quote: **...and the day of vengeance of our God; to comfort all who mourn** (Isa. 61:2).

Jesus left out the last portion because His First Advent was to establish the redemptive plan of God in the earth and bring His church into existence. The day of vengeance has not yet happened, and it will not happen until His Second Advent. The day of vengeance of our God will be at the Second Advent, the Battle of Armageddon.

But Isaiah did not see that, and neither did any of the Old Testament prophets. Jesus did not speak directly about it, but His earthly ministry, the First Advent, does provide a foreshadowing of His purpose.

Two Days With the Gentiles

In John 4, we have the account of Jesus' encounter with the Samaritan woman at the well. Jesus decided to travel from Judea to Galilee. On the way He passed through Samaria, which was a heathen nation. It was not a part of the commonwealth of Israel, the family of God.

On other occasions, Jesus encountered Gentiles and frequently would not offer ministry to them. You will recall from Matthew 15:22-28 the woman of Canaan who wanted Him to heal her daughter. He said, "No. I have come to minister to the Jews," but her faith moved Him to heal her daughter anyway.

So the Jews were the focus of the ministry during the First Advent. But in this trip from Judea to Galilee, we see a foreshadowing of His larger ministry. He ran into a woman at a well and, in the course of discussion, revealed to her who He was. She was excited when she realized He was the Messiah, so she left and brought all the villagers to see Him. They begged Jesus to stay with them, and He did so for two days. (John 4:40.)

That is significant to end-time theology. The Bible says in 2 Peter 3:8 not to be ignorant of the fact that, regarding end-time events, a day is as 1000 years and 1000 years is as a day. The Gentile church age interrupts the Jewish dispensation for 2000 years, just as Jesus interrupted His Jewish ministry for two days with the Gentiles.

We see the Gentile Samaritans' response to Jesus' ministry to them in John's gospel.

> **And many more believed because of His own word. Then they said to the woman, "Now we believe, not because of what you said, for we ourselves have heard Him and we know that this is indeed the Christ, the Savior of the world."**
>
> **John 4:41,42**

This is the birth of Christianity: the Gentiles' embracing Jesus as the Savior when the Jews rejected Him.

Then in verse 43, He went back to the Jews:

> **Now after the two days He departed from there and went to Galilee.**

This is a foreshadowing of the interruption of the Jewish dispensation between the sixty-ninth and seventieth weeks. The Gentiles received Him as the Christ and the church was born, but He will return to the Jews once again to complete His dealings with them. God is both amazingly consistent and consistently amazing.

No Old Testament prophet saw this. Not a one of them. That raises a question: "Why would the Lord not show it to somebody?" The answer is that the church age was intended to be a mystery.

In Ephesians 3, God tells us that no men in other ages knew about the mystery of the church age. It was not made known to them, as it is now unto His holy apostles and prophets.

> **If indeed you have heard of the dispensation of the grace of God which was given to me for you, how that by revelation He made known to me the mystery (as I have briefly written already, by which, when you read, you may understand my knowledge in the mystery of Christ), which in other ages was not made known to the sons of men, as it has now been revealed by the Spirit to His holy apostles and prophets: that the Gentiles should be fellow heirs, of the same body, and partakers of His promise in Christ through the gospel.**

> **Ephesians 3:2-6**

The Old Testament prophets saw right past the church age. Not having God's perspective on time, they would see from the First Advent straight into the Second Advent, as though it were all one.

It was also a mystery to Satan and the religious leaders whom he influenced to crucify Jesus.

> **But we speak the wisdom of God in a mystery, the hidden wisdom which God ordained before the ages for our glory, which none of the rulers of this age knew; for had they known, they would not have crucified the Lord of glory.**

> **1 Corinthians 2:7,8**

The greatest student of Scripture is Satan. He knows the Word thoroughly, and he listens to the prophets of God because his destiny hangs in the balance. If Satan had known what was going to be loosed on the kingdom of darkness, he would never have crucified the Lord of glory. So it was kept a mystery. That is why no Old Testament prophet, including Daniel, was enabled to see the church age.

The word *mystery* is defined as "closed (or unfruitful) to natural understanding or intellectual comprehension."[3] So how do you speak about something that is closed to intellectual comprehension? You speak by the Spirit.

> **For he who speaks in a tongue does not speak to men but to God, for no one understands him; however, in the spirit he speaks mysteries.**
>
> **1 Corinthians 14:2**

When you pray in tongues by the Holy Spirit, you are speaking mysteries about God's redemptive plan for man, because that is what the church age is, and God made it a mystery.

The mystery of God embraces the entire church age, of which you are a part and to which you are intended to make a contribution. Just as the crucifixion of Jesus was a mystery so that Satan would not know to avoid it, God's plan for your life is also a mystery to Satan.

If it were published, if it could be seen or heard, if man could conceive it, then the enemy of your soul would have powerful, advanced intelligence and do everything he could to keep it from happening.

So how do you get to the bottom of the mystery? God has revealed it to us by His Spirit, our teacher. **These things we also speak, not in words which man's wisdom teaches but which the Holy Spirit teaches, comparing spiritual things with spiritual** (1 Cor. 2:13).

The Holy Spirit's ministry to you is to reveal the mystery of God's plan for your life. That will happen as you yield to His indwelling presence. As you pray in the Spirit, you will find yourself receiving interpretation of your spiritual language, and spiritual truths will be revealed to you.

If the plan of God for your life is still a mystery to you, then one of two things is happening: Either you are not filled with the Spirit, or the time has not yet come for you to know His plan. Another possibility is that you are not praying in the Spirit, in which case you have no one to blame except yourself.

There is a fullness of time for most everything God does; it relates to our spiritual maturity and growth in the Word. If much of the mystery were revealed to us now, we probably could not handle it or we would misuse it or it would give the enemy of our souls an opportunity to stop it or delay it.

God does not usually reveal everything to us all at one time. It is a progressive process, and it relates to our commitment to the Word of God, to growing in the Lord, to pursuing God.

As you develop these spiritual disciplines in your life, more of the mystery will be revealed. You will be praying in the Spirit and you will have another dream, another flash of something God has shown you about your life.

The fact that He has shown it to you means you can handle it. God is not going to show you some things until you are mature enough spiritually to handle them. So when God reveals pieces of His plan for you, have a little faith. God would not show them to you unless together you and He can accomplish them.

CHAPTER SIXTEEN

The First Seal

The seven seals are the events which are going to occur on earth during the seven-year period called the Tribulation. When the Word talks about the book being unsealed, it is referring to the book of prophecy which has yet to be fulfilled during the Tribulation.

The first seal is broken in Revelation 6.

> **Now I saw when the Lamb opened one of the seals; and I heard one of the four living creatures saying with a voice like thunder, "Come and see." And I looked, and behold, a white horse. He who sat on it had a bow; and a crown was given to him, and he went out conquering and to conquer.**
>
> **Revelation 6:1,2**

Some scholars believe this is referring to Jesus. They reason that a white horse is always symbolic of the Lord and, therefore, this refers to His first coming.

But that explanation would not fit the chronology of the book of Revelation, which indicates how it is to be interpreted.

John was told to write first the things he had seen, then the things that are, then the things which are to come. From chapter 4 on, we are dealing with the **"things which must take place after this"** (v. 1). They have not occurred yet.

So the figure in the first seal has nothing to do with the First Advent of Jesus. Nor does it have to do with the Second Advent of Jesus, because that occurs in Revelation 19. There, He has thousands upon thousands of saints with Him. Additionally, unlike the one described in Revelation 6:2, Jesus' weapon is not a bow, but a sword.

The Antichrist

This passage from chapter 6 is the revelation of the Antichrist. And as we will see in a moment, this is the first thing that happens after the Rapture of the church. It begins the Tribulation.

The Antichrist comes looking like a good guy. He comes on a white horse. He comes wanting people to think he is Jesus, the Christ. He comes proclaiming to be *a* prince, if not *the* Prince, of peace. That is the good news he peddles. He sells people on the idea that he is the one who can solve all the world's problems and bring peace.

But the crown representing the Antichrist's authority has to be given to him. We will see later who will give it to him and how it will come to be his.

By contrast, Jesus wears a crown by virtue of who He is; no one had to give it to Him. His authority is invested in Him as the Son of God.

The Rapture and the Second Coming

Now, brethren, concerning the coming of our Lord Jesus Christ and our gathering together to Him, we ask you, not to be soon shaken in mind or troubled, either by spirit or by word or by letter, as if from us, as though the day of Christ had come.

2 Thessalonians 2:1,2

Here Paul refers to both the Second Advent and the Rapture. **Our gathering together to Him** is a reference to the Rapture. The young church at Thessalonica was a little concerned because they had been misinformed that the Second Advent was at hand. But Paul goes on to explain:

> **Let no one deceive you by any means; for that Day will not come unless the falling away comes first, and the man of sin is revealed, the son of perdition.**
>
> **2 Thessalonians 2:3**

The Greek word *apostasia* is a combination of the root words *ago*, meaning "away," and *histinai*, which means "to stand." Thus we have "one who stands away," or departs.[1] This preferred translation is clearly a reference to the Rapture and fits the chronology of Revelation exactly.

That Day, the Second Advent, will be proceeded first by the Rapture of the church and then by the revealing of **the man of sin...the son of perdition.** So two things happen before the Second Advent: The church is raptured and the man of sin, or the Antichrist, is revealed.

And now you know what is restraining, that he may be revealed in his own time. There is something withholding the revelation of the Antichrist. **For the mystery of lawlessness is already at work; only He who now restrains will do so until He is taken out of the way** (2 Thess. 2:6,7).

This is saying sin is already at work in the earth, but the ultimate revelation of the Antichrist is being withheld. This is talking about an entity in the earth today which makes it impossible for the pure evil that is antichrist to be fully manifest. That entity opposing evil is the church!

There is already a spirit of antichrist at work in the earth right now, promoting the kinds of wicked behavior we see all over the world today. But it is being restrained. The church is the force in the earth restraining the full loosing of that spirit of lawlessness in the earth.

But not every part of the church is doing its part in this effort. Dead, lifeless fellowships mired in tradition and religiosity offer no resistance at all to the devil. These powerless churches are the ones without any life of the Spirit within them; they are not bastions of prayer. Why should Satan fear them? They represent little or no threat to his efforts.

It is the Spirit-filled church endued with power from on high, as we see in the book of Acts, which is the greatest force in the earth today, keeping lawlessness from manifesting without restraint.

No wise civil servant, no governor or king has ever been able to orchestrate the peace which is in the earth, nor have they been able to keep evil from being manifest. It is not our cherished laws or legal system which has restrained the devil's hand.

The reason things have not gone "to hell in a hand basket" already is that the church has yielded to the Spirit of God in prayer. That is what holds the force of darkness at bay. Therefore, the man of sin, the Antichrist, cannot be revealed until the church is taken out of the earth.

Until the Rapture of the church occurs, you can forget all of this nonsense about who the Antichrist is or whether he is here already, because who he is will not be revealed until the church is out of here.

The Seventieth Week Begins

Following the Rapture of the church comes the Tribulation, Daniel's Seventieth Week.

"Then [the Antichrist] **shall confirm a covenant with many for one week; but in the middle of the week He shall bring an end to sacrifice and offering. And on the wing of abominations shall be one who makes desolate, even until the consummation, which is determined, is poured out on the desolate."**

Daniel 9:27

The first thing we see happening is that the Antichrist will **"confirm a covenant with many for one week."** How long is one week? Seven years. Also, notice he will confirm *a* covenant, not *the* covenant. This is not the same covenant we have with the Lord. The "many" with whom he will confirm this covenant are the Jews.

In the midst of the week, or at the three-and-a-half year mark, **He shall bring an end to sacrifice and offering.** As there is presently no temple nor any sacrificing being done, this means that sometime between now and the revelation of the Antichrist, or with the initiation of his covenant, there will be a temple built in Jerusalem and sacrifices resumed.

But in the middle of his seven-year covenant, the Antichrist will go back on his word. He will break his covenant and stop the sacrifices and offerings.

"And on the wing of abominations shall be one who makes desolate, even until the consummation, which is determined, is poured out on the desolate."

Daniel 9:27

This is when a terrible time in the life of Israel will begin. The children of Israel will come under severe persecution lasting until the Battle of Armageddon, when the full, predetermined end is manifest.

For the first three and a half years, the Antichrist will have been busy consolidating his power base among the ten-nation confederacy, which he ultimately will head up. And he will have been resting comfortably on the security of the covenant he has in place, which declares him to be a man of both national and world peace. He deceives many with this strategy.

It is really not that different from the peace pact Adolf Hitler made with Russia prior to invading France. He only honored that pact until he had finalized his purposes on the Western Front; then he broke his pact and attacked Russia.

It will be the same with Antichrist; Hitler was operating by that same spirit. The Antichrist will use the peace pact only as long as it serves his purposes.

Then the true colors will begin to show. He will break his covenant with Israel. He will stop the sacrifices and offerings and launch a heavy assault on the children of God who have trusted in Jesus since the Rapture. His purpose will be to defeat Christ, but at the battle of Armageddon, he himself will be defeated.

The Great Tribulation

The first five seals we find in Revelation 6 occur during the first three-and-a-half years of the Tribulation. They happen because that lawless spirit, the mystery of iniquity, will be on a rampage with nothing to restrain it, nothing to hold it back.

But in the second three and a half years, not only will the people on the earth have to contend with unrestrained evil, but they also will have to contend with the Antichrist, who will then be pursuing a very determined agenda to eradicate the plan of God and defeat Christ. That is why the last three-and-a-half years are called **the *great* tribulation** (Rev. 7:14).

Origin of the Antichrist

We can see the origin of the Antichrist in Daniel 7. God reveals to Daniel four great empires which will arise, beginning with the Babylonian Empire. After Babylon's fall there is the Medo-Persian Empire, then the Grecian Empire and finally the Roman Empire.

We see a reference to this in verse 23.

"Thus he said: 'The fourth beast shall be a fourth kingdom on earth, which shall be *different from all other kingdoms,* and shall devour the whole earth, trample it and break it in pieces.'"

Daniel 7:23

The Roman Empire *was* different from all the other kingdoms. It was the first empire to cover all of the known world, trampling it down. Eventually, with the breakup of the Roman Empire itself, the world broke into pieces.

The Rise of the Roman Empire

"The ten horns are ten kings who shall arise from this kingdom. And another shall rise after them; he shall be different from the first ones, and shall subdue three kings."

Daniel 7:24

This is a revelation of what is to come. Ten kings, or ten nations, will rise out of the old Roman Empire. Most scholars agree this is the ten-nation confederacy represented by the European Common Market.

Greece became a member in 1981, making the European Common Market a ten-nation confederacy. The area it covers is identical to the geographical location of the old Roman Empire. While the membership of the European Common Market can fluctuate, I can assure you that by the time the Rapture of the church occurs, there will be ten members.

But out of this ten-king confederacy another will rise. This is the Antichrist. He will subdue three of the kingdoms, or nations, in the Common Market. This will occur during the first three-and-a-half years of the Tribulation when the Antichrist will be consolidating his power base in the ten-nation confederacy.

The physical subjection of three of the nations in the ten-nation confederacy will be his way of demonstrating his power in order to force the rest of the nations to fall in line behind him.

Persecution of the Saints

Then the Antichrist's true colors will begin to show. After three and a half years, a dramatic shift will take place.

"He shall speak pompous words against the Most High, shall persecute the saints of the Most High, and shall intend to change times and law. Then the saints shall be given into his hand for a time and times and half a time."

Daniel 7:25

"Time and times and half a time" refers to the second half of the Tribulation.

The Antichrist's initial strategy will be to present himself as a man of peace; but once his power base is complete, he will feel free to execute his true intentions. In Daniel 8:24, we see that his power will be great, but it will not come from him. He will get his power from another source—Satan.

**"His power shall be mighty, but not by his own power;
he shall destroy fearfully, and shall prosper and thrive; he
shall destroy the mighty, and also the holy people. Through
his cunning he shall cause deceit to prosper under his rule;
and he shall exalt himself in his heart. He shall destroy many
in their prosperity. He shall even rise against the Prince of
princes; but he shall be broken without human means."**

Daniel 8:24,25

Craftiness, or deception, will be a part of the Antichrist's reign. He will even become convinced he is the one the world should worship.

Signs of His Coming

In Matthew 24:3 the disciples ask Jesus about the end times: What would the signs of His coming and the end of the world be? Keep in mind Jesus was talking here to Jews, not to the church. He was not talking about the signs of His coming for the church at the Rapture, but of His coming for the Jews at the end of the Jewish dispensation. Remember, the entire church age was still a mystery at this point.

People wrongly say, "There are wars and rumors of wars, famines, pestilence and earthquakes, so we must be in that day. The signs are here. The Lord must be coming." No. These are not signs of the Rapture. These are signs of the Second Advent.

What you actually see in Matthew 24 is another view of six of the seven seals of Revelation 6 and 7. Jesus was giving a view of the Tribulation period, the seven years which will lead up to the Second Advent. These, then, are the signs of His *second* coming and the end of the Jewish dispensation.

**"Then two men will be in the field: one will be taken
and the other left. Two women will be grinding at the mill:
one will be taken and the other left.**

**"Watch therefore, for you do not know what hour your
Lord is coming."**

Matthew 24:40-42

With this passage as inpiration, sad songs have been sung about people being left at the Rapture, but actually this is Jesus telling the Jews the way it will be at His Second Advent. If you read these verses in the context of the previous ones, it becomes clear:

"But as the days of Noah were, so also will the coming of the Son of Man be. For as in the days before the flood, they were eating and drinking, marrying and giving in marriage, until the day that Noah entered the ark, and did not know until the flood came and took them all away, so also will the coming of the Son of Man be."

Matthew 24:37-39

God took the ones in the ark out of harm's way, but the Flood took the lives of those who remained. The Word says the coming of the Son of Man will be the same way. Of those who have not gone away in the "ark" of the Rapture, two of *them* will be in the field; one will be taken, the other left. One will be killed, the other will not.

This is not a Rapture Scripture; rather, this is describing the persecution by the Antichrist, the judgment after the Rapture, during the end of the Jewish dispensation.

Jesus Prophesies the First Seal

Matthew 24:4 is a picture of the first seal being opened. The first thing Jesus says about the end times is the same as what Revelation 6:2 says about the first seal.

And Jesus answered and said to them: "Take heed that no one deceives you. For many will come in My name, saying, 'I am the Christ,' and will deceive many."

Matthew 24:4,5

The Antichrist will ride on a white horse claiming to be the harbinger of peace, letting people think he is the Christ. He will ride up looking like a good guy, only to deceive many.

The first seal loosed in the earth in Revelation is the spirit of deception. The Antichrist is the manifestation of that deception, because he is received as a man of peace.

And remember what 1 Thessalonians 5:3 says: **For when they say, "Peace and safety!" then sudden destruction comes upon them.**

What we must understand is that this same spirit is in the earth today, laboring to promote deception among the body of Christ. This deception will only fully manifest after the Rapture of the church.

The Antichrist will not put on another hat. His tactics will remain the same. The only difference is the church, the hinderer of lawlessness, will no longer be in his way. The strategy is the same: deceive through feigned promotion of peace.

The Strategy of Deception

The reason this is so dangerous is that the Word says we are to follow after peace. Yet the Antichrist uses peace as the primary ploy to bring deception to the people who love God.

Why has Satan staked everything on this strategy of deception? The truth is that if the devil cannot deceive you, he cannot defeat you. It has been that way since the Garden of Eden.

God does not transgress your free moral agency by imposing His will on you for good. He is certainly not going to allow the devil to impose his will on you for evil.

Satan's only weapon is to deceive you into making wrong choices. God says in Deuteronomy 30:19, **"I have set before you life and death, blessing and cursing; therefore choose life, that both you and your descendants may live."**

Your experience of blessing or cursing really can be traced back to the choices you have made. The only way you can experience evil at the hand of the enemy of your soul is if he can deceive you into making wrong choices through ignorance, misinformation or religious tradition.

You have to understand the importance of knowing the truth, because only the truth can set you free from deception. If the enemy cannot deceive you, he cannot defeat you. His strategy in using deception in the body of Christ will only be fully manifest after the body of Christ is raptured; nevertheless, it is among us today.

An Inaccurate Definition of Peace

The Antichrist will deceive the whole world by promoting peace, but the kind of peace he will promote is simply the absence of conflict, which is how many people define peace. Most people think of peace as nothing more than nations or armies calling a cease-fire and laying down their weapons—a mere absence of conflict.

This "peace" is vastly different from the peace of God, which is to lead the believer. Many people in the body of Christ think the gospel message of peace is this "no conflict" kind of peace. But it is not.

Yes, we are to be peacemakers, but if we wrongly define peace using the world's definition, which is ultimately the Antichrist's definition, we allow the deception of the Antichrist in. We will also experience significant defeat in our lives and the life of the church because of it.

This false definition of peace as the absence of conflict has given the body of Christ a wimpy, turn-the-other-cheek, let-the-world-walk-all-over-us kind of image. Anyone with an ounce of boldness and an inch of backbone would not want to be associated with that!

God's Peace

God's definition of peace is quite different from the Antichrist's. You cannot define the peace of God in natural terms, and it is certainly *not* the mere absence of conflict.

So how do we follow the peace of God? If the peace we pursue cannot be defined in natural terms, what is the peace of God?

The peace we are to follow after cannot be logically or intellectually justified, understood or rationalized. It defies all natural understanding, but what it does do is keep your heart and mind at peace. It brings a tranquillity that no storm of life can disturb. It is the God-kind of peace.

And the peace of God, which surpasses all understanding, will guard your hearts and minds through Christ Jesus.

Philippians 4:7

CHAPTER SEVENTEEN

The Seven Seals

I want to emphasize the fact that the first five seals in Revelation 6 have nothing to do with the wrath of God. The wrath of God is not poured out until the sixth seal. The first five seals are events which will happen on planet earth solely because the church is gone.

The Second Seal

When He opened the second seal, I heard the second living creature saying, "Come and see." Another horse, fiery red, went out. And it was granted to the one who sat on it to take peace from the earth, and that people should kill one another; and there was given to him a great sword.

Revelation 6:3,4

A notable change in social behavior will take place after the Rapture of the church and the revelation of the Antichrist. Conflict resolution will no longer be possible without bloodshed. Therefore, there will be a rapid spread of armed conflict, war—which is what the sword in the above passage refers to—on a global scale. So the second seal is war, killing and the resolution of conflict only through bloodshed.

It will not be just nation against nation, but city against city, community against community and neighbor against neighbor. It will be warfare on a scale never experienced before by human beings, because, with the church gone, there will no longer be any restraint against violence to resolve conflict.

The Third Seal

When He opened the third seal, I heard the third living creature say, "Come and see." So I looked, and behold, a black horse, and he who sat on it had a pair of scales in his hand. And I heard a voice in the midst of the four living creatures saying, "A quart of wheat for a denarius, and three quarts of barley for a denarius; and do not harm the oil and the wine."

Revelation 6:5,6

The third seal is famine. At this point in time, a penny will be a day's wages. A person will have to labor an entire day just to get two handfuls of wheat.

There will be extreme financial crisis in the earth. When the world is at war and all the resources, both human and natural, are being given over to the production of weapons, war materials and supplies, the natural economy will be the victim.

Agricultural production will fall severely low because everybody will be in the army fighting the war and no one will be working the fields. Everyone will be too busy killing his neighbors. With no attention or resources given to economic and farm production, famine will follow.

History has proven this time and time again. When there is war on a global scale, invariably a good portion of the world is involved in some sort of economic recession, or financial crisis. The Bible calls it famine.

That is what is happening in Russia right now. For decades, Russia poured all of her natural resources into the production of war materials and defense, and the economy just fell apart. Today they are struggling with a severe financial crisis; famine is in the land.

We see this pattern throughout history, and we will see it once again on a much larger scale during the seven-year Tribulation period.

The Fourth Seal

When He opened the fourth seal, I heard the voice of the fourth living creature saying, "Come and see." So I looked, and behold, a pale horse. And the name of him who sat on it was Death, and Hades followed with him. And power was given to them over a fourth of the earth, to kill with sword, with hunger, with death, and by the beasts of the earth.

Revelation 6:7,8

It is not quite as clear here as Jesus makes it in Matthew, but the fourth seal is described as pestilence—the death which follows the other three seals. Without Jesus, where does death take you? To hell. So hell follows Death when he rides, and it affects a fourth of the population of earth.

It is a pattern we see throughout human history. The Dark Ages are a terrifying example: The Black Death swept the world as death touched the human population to a degree never before known. One out of every eight people at that time died. It followed a time in which feudal warfare was commonplace, a time in which little kingdoms battled each other constantly.

Famine became a factor. Then pestilence, in the form of the bubonic plague carried by rats, was a result of all of the dead lying in the fields after the armies had battled. The famine killed; then the rats came, and pestilence became a factor in the spread of disease. Finally, the death toll was beyond anything experienced till that point.

We see this exact same progression prophesied about the Tribulation. It will begin with war—the inability to resolve conflict without shedding blood; then severe financial collapse and crisis will lead to famine; then pestilence and disease will come. Death will be so widespread that a fourth of the people on the planet will die. That amounts to *billions* of deaths.

Never before has anything like this been seen.

The Fifth Seal

When He opened the fifth seal, I saw under the altar the souls of those who had been slain for the word of God and for the testimony which they held. And they cried with a loud voice, saying, "How long, O Lord, holy and true, until You judge and avenge our blood on those who dwell on the earth?"

Then a white robe was given to each of them; and it was said to them that they should rest a little while longer, until both the number of their fellow servants and their brethren, who would be killed as they were, was completed.

Revelation 6:9-11

The fifth seal is the loosing of the persecution against the believers who are alive on the earth during the Tribulation. The Antichrist will launch a systematic persecution against these believers. That is what the mark of the Beast will be all about. The only way out will be death; if one will not deny the faith, then he or she will be martyred.

You can see this in verse 11: **...they should rest a little while longer, until both the number of their fellow servants and their brethren, who would be killed as they were, was completed.** The implication is clear: If you are a believer during the Tribulation, the only way out will be martyrdom.

How will there be believers here during the Tribulation after the church is raptured? First of all, a lot of people will get saved when the church is raptured. A good portion of the earth will sit up and take notice when hundreds of millions of people suddenly disappear with no explanation.

There is going to be a real harvest of people coming into the kingdom. Young people will say, "This is what my grandma talked about; and I laughed at her, but it really happened." They are going to get saved.

Secondly, there will be people who know what the Bible says but have never committed, and they are going to become Tribulation believers.

What is loosed by the fifth seal is the persecution which brings about martyrdom for those that become believers after the Rapture.

The Sixth Seal

The opening of the first five seals will be a result of the church's being taken out of the earth. Then the opening of the sixth seal will begin the outpouring of God's wrath.

I looked when He opened the sixth seal, and behold, there was a great earthquake; and the sun became black as sackcloth of hair, and the moon became like blood. And the stars of heaven fell to the earth, as a fig tree drops its late figs when it is shaken by a mighty wind.

Then the sky receded as a scroll when it is rolled up, and every mountain and island was moved out of its place. And the kings of the earth, the great men, the rich men, the commanders, the mighty men, every slave and every free man, hid themselves in the caves and in the rocks of the mountains.

Revelation 6:12-15

What we see here is the beginning of the outpouring of God's wrath. The sixth seal will probably occur after the midpoint of the Tribulation, after three-and-a-half years, and begin the last three-and-a-half years of the Tribulation, called "The Great Tribulation."

The Antichrist will break his covenant with Israel, which will be the only thing restraining God's hand. Then he will begin to actively pursue the children of God and persecute them. At the same time, God will begin pouring out His wrath upon this earth.

Jesus' Teaching on the Six Seals

All six seals we just studied in Revelation 6 are discernable in the discourse Jesus gives His disciples in Matthew 24.

And Jesus answered and said to them: "Take heed that no one deceives you. For many will come in My name, saying, 'I am the Christ,' and will deceive many."

Matthew 24:4

This is the first seal, the coming of the Antichrist.

"And you will hear of wars and rumors of wars. See that you are not troubled; for all these things must come to pass, but the end is not yet."

Matthew 24:6

This is the second seal, the conflicts which can only be resolved by bloodshed.

"For nation will rise against nation, and kingdom against kingdom. And there will be famines [the third seal] pestilences, and earthquakes in various places."

Matthew 24:7

The consummation of the wars and famine and pestilence, and of course death, is the fourth seal.

"Then they will deliver you up to tribulation and kill you, and you will be hated by all nations for My name's sake."

Matthew 24:9

Here we have the persecution and martyrdom—the fifth seal.

Jesus also discusses the Antichrist's breaking of the covenant with the nation of Israel at the midpoint of the Tribulation—three-and-a-half years into it:

"Therefore when you see the 'abomination of desolation,' spoken of by Daniel the prophet, standing in the holy place" —whoever reads, let him understand), "then let those who are in Judea flee to the mountains. Let him who is on the housetop not go down to take anything out of his house. And let him who is in the field not go back to get his clothes. But woe to those who are pregnant and to those who are nursing babies in those days! And pray that your flight may not be in winter or on the Sabbath."

Matthew 24:15-20

God, the Righteous Judge

And the kings of the earth, the great men, the rich men, the commanders, the mighty men, every slave and every free man, hid themselves in the caves and in the rocks of the mountains, and said to the mountains and rocks, "Fall on us and hide us from the face of Him who sits on the throne and from the wrath of the Lamb! For the great day of His wrath has come, and who is able to stand?"

Revelation 6:15-17

Most believers are woefully ignorant regarding the matter of judgment. When something bad happens to them, they do not know whether it is caused by the devil or it is God judging them for something. They look at things like the taking of the firstborn of Egypt, and they say, "How could God do that to innocent little babies? Do I really serve a loving, merciful heavenly Father if He can kill babies?"

When Joshua was leading the children of Israel into the Promised Land, God told Joshua each time they came to a village, "Kill them all. Men, women, babies, even their livestock. Slaughter every living thing."

People say to themselves, "How could this order be from a loving, merciful heavenly Father? I just do not understand."

I have heard people say about the Tribulation, "I really do not know whether to believe all of that or not. The Bible says I serve a God of love, whose mercy endures forever, so I do not know if it is really going to be like that. I just cannot believe that He is going to cause all that suffering."

We *must* understand what the judgment of God is all about. The word *judgment* means "the imposition of justice by verdict."[1] If the verdict is guilt, justice is imposed through penalty. If the verdict is innocence, justice is imposed by blessing.

This relates to the laws governing the very fabric of life in this universe as we know it, as given to us through the Bible. Those laws are going to be fulfilled and lived by; or if they are broken, there will be a penalty to be paid.

There is a spiritual law which undergirds every experience of life. The natural, physical laws—the laws of gravity, of motion, of energy—are nothing more than an extension of the spiritual laws dictated by God, which control this universe.

God and His Word are one. He has no choice but to execute the law which is a part of His very Being and which He brought into existence. So it is not a matter of being unmerciful. All of creation would be unbalanced if He did not execute the laws He established. It is a matter of His sustaining the integrity of creation, which came into existence by His Word and His law.

Penalty or Blessing

Judgment is the meting out of justice; it is seeing to it that the law is fulfilled either by blessing or by penalty. Judgment occurs in two arenas: the temporal arena and the eternal arena.

We see the temporal arena in Deuteronomy 28 in the form of the law. Judgment either brings blessing or cursing, depending on how you relate it to the law of God. The first thing discussed here in Deuteronomy 28 is blessing. If you hearken diligently to all of His commandments—to the Word of the Lord—then you will be blessed, and the list of blessings runs all the way down to verse 13. This passage is summarized by saying the Lord will make us the head and not the tail, above and not beneath—but only if we obey the Word of the Lord.

Now, the other side of justice is dealt with in verse 15, in which He tells us that if we do not obey, all of these curses will come on us. Then He lists all the curses. There are curses which involve the loss of family and loved ones, relationship deterioration and poverty. Deuteronomy 28:61 summarizes by saying that every sickness and plague written in this book, the Lord will bring on you until you are destroyed.

Judgment is *not* the fist of God coming down in retribution, even though that is the way most people see it.

Because of their view of God, the *King James Version* translators rendered all of the Old Testament Hebrew verbs in the *causative* rather than the *permissive* sense, even though either tense is linguistically possible. (Such verb tenses don't even exist in the Hebrew language.)

The translators *assumed* the verbs were in the causative tense because it was the way they assumed God operated.

It's important to understand that it is not the translations which are divinely inspired. It is the original texts in the original language which are God-breathed, inerrant and infallible.

A translation can be sponsored by a sect or denomination which interprets the Scripture in a way which is highly favorable to their persuasion.

I believe many of the Hebrew verbs describing God's activity in the Old Testament *should* be translated in the permissive sense. In the causative sense, a verse might read, "The Lord will cause." But, in the permissive sense it would say, "The Lord will permit [because it is your choice]."

When you obey, you are under the umbrella of His protection. When you disobey, you move out from under His protection, and He has no choice but to allow the curse, which is already in the earth because of sin, to touch your life.

Judgment in the Spiritual Realm

Judgment will also occur in the internal, or spiritual, realm for the believer at the judgment seat of Christ and for the unbeliever at the Great White Throne judgment.

Many Christians today say, "The blood of Jesus has cleansed me from all unrighteousness. Jesus paid the price for my sin, and therefore I do not have to pay the penalty. Judgment is not an issue for me."

That is true, but only if from the time of your salvation you never sinned again. When you get saved, your past is eradicated, but the law of God still makes it necessary for us to conform our lives to His standard if we want to avoid future judgment.

So in our lives as Christians, if sin and disobedience is a continuing fact of our lives, then we are in line for judgment unless we confess and repent.

So when you make a mistake, you are in line for judgment unless you confess and repent and draw on the enabling power of the Holy Spirit within you to make that change.

Then you are cleansed from unrighteousness once more. You are free of the prospect of judgment in the negative sense, because the blood has been applied. But if you do not confess and repent, you are in line for judgment and will suffer the penalty of the law, the curse of the law.

The Bible says we are redeemed from the curse of the law, but only if we go to Jesus for that redemption. No matter what your sin may be, do not run from God. Do not be so ashamed that you hide from God as Adam did. God loves you. Run to Him, and tell Him you are sorry and you are not going to do it again; and the Holy Spirit will help you keep your word.

I sometimes hear unbelievers say, "Why do I need to get saved? Look at that guy; he is about as bad as anyone can get, and look at how rich he is and how well he is doing! There is no penalty for living wrong."

Do not be deceived! That is the mercy of God. But the day is coming when the books are going to be balanced, because He is a just God, and there is no other way for it to be.

That is really what the Tribulation is all about. It is not God just wiping out everything and everybody who has ever been ugly about Him. No. For thousands of years He has been merciful to mankind in spite of our ignorance and mockery of Him and in spite of the abominable things we have done. But that will end with the Tribulation. The mercy will end, and the judgment will come.

CHAPTER EIGHTEEN

The 144,000 Evangelists

With the opening of the sixth seal at the end of Revelation 6, we see the judgment of God begin. Many of the chapters between chapters 6 and 20 do not introduce new events but rather serve to amplify the events summarized in chapter 6.

Chapter 6 is an account of the events that will occur up until the Day of the Lord, but it is a very brief summary. Chapter 7 goes on to amplify.

> **After these things I saw four angels standing at the four corners of the earth, holding the four winds of the earth, that the wind should not blow on the earth, on the sea, or on any tree. Then I saw another angel ascending from the east, having the seal of the living God. And he cried with a loud voice to the four angels to whom it was granted to harm the earth and the sea, saying, "Do not harm the earth, the sea, or the trees till we have sealed the servants of our God on their foreheads." And I heard the number of those who were sealed. One hundred and**

forty-four thousand of all the tribes of the children of Israel were sealed.

Revelation 7:1-4

The next four verses talk about 12,000 coming out of each of the twelve tribes of Israel. However, there is one tribe not listed here—the tribe of Dan. Dan is not one of the tribes which is sealed, because the people of that tribe continually engaged in idol worship and were often the first to move away from God and backslide after repentance.

As the Millennium begins, Israel will watch the event unfold. However, her people will not be part of the sealing, except for the 144,000 Jewish evangelists.

The White-Robed Crowd

After these things I looked, and behold, a great multitude which no one could number, of all nations, tribes, peoples, and tongues, standing before the throne and before the Lamb, clothed with white robes, with palm branches in their hands, and crying out with a loud voice, saying, "Salvation belongs to our God who sits on the throne, and to the Lamb!" All the angels stood around the throne and the elders and the four living creatures, and fell on their faces before the throne and worshiped God, saying: "Amen! Blessing and glory and wisdom, thanksgiving and honor and power and might, be to our God forever and ever. Amen."

Then one of the elders answered, saying to me, "Who are these arrayed in white robes, and where did they come from?" And I said to him, "Sir, you know." So he said to me, "These are the ones who come out of the great tribulation, and washed their robes and made them white in the blood of the Lamb. Therefore they are before the throne of God, and serve Him day and night in His temple. And He who sits on the throne will dwell among them. They shall neither hunger

anymore nor thirst anymore; the sun shall not strike them, nor any heat; for the Lamb who is in the midst of the throne will shepherd them and lead them to living fountains of waters. And God will wipe away every tear from their eyes."

Revelation 7:9-17

This is an amplification of chapter 6, where John saw the souls of those who were slain for the Word of God and for the testimony which they held under the altar. They asked God how long it would be till they were avenged, and God told them to rest until all of the others would be martyred.

These in Revelation 7:14 are the same people. They are the ones who come out of the Great Tribulation. These are the Tribulation saints, or believers.

Many will be saved as a result of the Rapture. When the church goes and millions of people disappear, it is going to have a profound effect on many of those who remain. That is why God seals 144,000 Jewish men: for the purpose of evangelism.

The result is another great harvest of souls coming into the kingdom of God. Verse 9 says, **after these things.** After what things? After the sealing of the 144,000, John saw a great multitude, **which no one could number.** A great harvest of souls will come in as a result of the work of those 144,000 Jewish evangelists.

Now, there are cults which teach weird things about the 144,000. There is a group called "The Manifested Sons of God" who teach that only 144,000 are going to go to heaven. How you become one of them no one really seems to know. There are others, such as the Jehovah's Witnesses, who believe somewhat the same.

However sincere they are in their beliefs, they are sincerely wrong. The Scripture clearly contradicts what they teach.

First of all, this event takes place in the *hereafter.* Remember, Jesus told John to write things he had seen, things that are now and things that will be hereafter.

Things John had seen were taken care of in chapter 1. The things which are were covered in the letters to the churches. Then, *after* the church is raptured and this age is over, we are in the things that are hereafter. That is where this entrance of the 144,000 occurs, and the church will already be gone at this point.

So if somebody is claiming he is or you can be one of the 144,000 now, he simply does not realize that the sealing of these folks will not occur until *after* the church is raptured.

A second reason is also clear: The 144,000 who will be sealed will be Jewish men from the tribes of Israel. Unless you or the person talking to you is a direct descendant of one of the listed tribes of Israel on the mother's side, it would be impossible to be among the 144,000.

Then I looked, and behold, a Lamb standing on Mount Zion, and with Him one hundred and forty-four thousand, having His Father's name written on their foreheads. And I heard a voice from heaven, like the voice of many waters, and like the voice of loud thunder. And I heard the sound of harpists playing their harps. They sang as it were a new song before the throne, before the four living creatures, and the elders; and no one could learn that song except the hundred and forty-four thousand who were redeemed from the earth. These are the ones who were not defiled with women, for they are virgins. These are the ones who follow the Lamb wherever He goes. These were redeemed from among men, being firstfruits to God and to the Lamb. And in their mouth was found no deceit, for they are without fault before the throne of God.

Revelation 14:1-5

We also see that they are all single men. This is at a period of time when the Antichrist reigns supreme and his spirit is throughout the earth. Yet their walks of holiness as ones **not defiled with women** make them witnesses for the Lord Jesus.

Now, I want you to see how they leave the earth, because it is different than what we see for other Tribulation believers. The only way out of the Tribulation for a believer is martyrdom. But that is not true for this group; they are the exception.

Now a great sign appeared in heaven: a woman clothed with the sun, with the moon under her feet, and on her head a garland of twelve stars.

Revelation 12:1

The woman described in this verse is the nation of Israel. The twelve stars on her head are the twelve tribes, from each of which 12,000 were taken.

Then being with child, she cried out in labor and in pain to give birth.

Revelation 12:2

This is during the Tribulation period.

She bore a male Child who was to rule all nations with a rod of iron. And her Child was caught up to God and His throne.

Revelation 12:5

We just read that the 144,000 are all men, and this is referring to the Jewish evangelists who were sealed in chapter 7. These are the ones whom the nation of Israel will bring forth during the Tribulation.

To rule all nations with a rod of iron is simply a reference to a truth which applies to any believer. We are going to rule and reign with Jesus. There are other parts of the Scripture which use this same terminology.

A rod of iron does not imply a harsh or dictatorial kind of rule or suppression of some sort. It refers to an unbending, uncompromising position. Part of ruling and reigning with Him is obedience to the law of God, which will be unbending. It will be unyielding and true for everyone on this earth, and it will be enforced impartially.

Peace will prevail. It will be a time of peace, so it will not be an imposition of rule on anyone, even though the terminology makes it sound that way.

Exit Stage "Up"

But I want you to see how the woman leaves the earth. Scripture says her child will be caught up to God and His throne. This occurs at the midpoint of the Tribulation. The 144,000 are going to evangelize the earth for three-and-a-half years and then get caught up to God. They will not die.

The Greek word translated *caught up* is the same word used to describe the Rapture in other places[1]—the act of being caught away to be with the Lord without experiencing physical death on this earth.

Those who would suggest there may be a mid-Tribulation Rapture should realize it is just for the 144,000. When these men finish their evangelism and multitudes more have come to God, then they will be caught up out of the earth just as the end-time church will have previously been caught up in the Rapture.

All the other believers are going to get out of the Tribulation by holding on to their faith until the end or by being martyred.

Chapter 20 talks about the ones who are saved because of the 144,000, the Tribulation saints.

> **And I saw thrones, and they sat on them, and judgment was committed to them. And I saw the souls of those who had been beheaded for their witness to Jesus and for the word of God, who had not worshipped the beast or his image, and had not received his mark on their foreheads or on their hands. And they lived and reigned with Christ for a thousand years.**
>
> **Revelation 20:4**

This verse is a direct reference to the millennial reign of Christ, and here John is talking about the martyrs who come out of the Tribulation.

Notice that he saw their souls. They were not raptured. Their bodies were not caught away as in the Rapture. He just saw their souls because they will not get their glorified bodies until Jesus establishes His earthly reign.

Two Resurrections

> **But the rest of the dead did not live again until the thousand years were finished. This is the first resurrection.**
>
> **Revelation 20:5**

At the end of the 1000-year reign of Christ, there are two resurrections. The first resurrection is for those who have become believers during the Tribulation. But if there is a first resurrection, what is the second?

> **Then I saw a great white throne and Him who sat on it, from whose face the earth and the heaven fled away. And there was found no place for them. And I saw the dead, small and great, standing before God, and books were opened. And another book was opened, which is the Book of Life. And the dead were judged according to their works, by the things which were written in the books.**
>
> **The sea gave up the dead who were in it, and Death and Hades delivered up the dead who were in them. And they were judged, each one according to his works. Then Death and Hades were cast into the lake of fire. This is the second death. And anyone not found written in the Book of Life was cast into the lake of fire.**
>
> **Revelation 20:11-15**

This second resurrection is the resurrection of the unbelievers to stand before the Great White Throne, and they will experience something called the second death.

God's Emphasis on Evangelism

I want you to notice the emphasis, the importance, God places on evangelism. In the midst of the greatest outpouring of God's wrath and judgment this world will ever see, He will still send 144,000 evangelists into the world to win as many as He can into the kingdom of God—even in the last moments.

The Word shows us repeatedly that it is not God's will that any should perish. Even during this period of time—a time reserved since the fall of Adam for the judgment and the justice of God to be worked out in the earth—God is interested in bringing as many souls into the kingdom as possible, and He seals the 144,000 evangelists to accomplish that end.

Evangelism is the heart of God today as much as it will be then. God is the same yesterday, today and forever. (Heb. 13:8.) For us as a church alive in this dispensation, this is our commission: to be used of God in any way possible to bring the lost into the kingdom of God.

When your light shines for Jesus, you are an evangelist. So I would suggest that a good measuring rod for your life would be your answer to this question: Do you share the Lord freely, willingly and frequently as He gives you the opportunities, or do you tend to shy away from that responsibility? You cannot obey the Word of God and keep Jesus all to yourself.

We all have two calls in common which transcend all boundaries and denominational lines. One is our call to be God's stewards. We are here to rule and reign with Him, to manage and administrate the resources of this life on His behalf. Everything belongs to the Lord.

The second call is the mandate to share the Good News with others so they can be saved. That is the heart of God. Your response to this call is a measure of how well you are obeying the Word of God. Your life should affect somebody else for Jesus Christ.

Power and Purpose

The *power* of God does not flow independently of the *purpose* of God. Many Christians are after the power of God today and are wondering where it is. But His power is right there, ready and waiting to accomplish His purposes in the earth.

What is the purpose of God for your life? Only when you align your life with His purpose can you expect the power to flow. God is not going to empower you to pursue your own private agenda, no matter how noble you may think it is. It is only when you align your life with the purpose of God—the salvation of the lost—that you can expect the power to flow.

God's power is not intended to entertain, to give you goose bumps or to deliver you from whatever your introverted need may be. That may shock you. He loves us as a heavenly Father. He wants us to be healed and provided for, but that is not the *purpose* of His power in our lives.

In Acts 1:8 we see very clearly what the purpose is.

"But you shall receive power when the Holy Spirit has come upon you; and you shall be witnesses to Me in Jerusalem, and in all Judea and Samaria, and to the end of the earth."

God's power and purpose are forever linked together. He does not say, "You shall receive power after the Holy Spirit has come upon you; and you will be healed, delivered, set free, prosperous and able to retire early..." No. You will receive power after the Holy Spirit has come on you to evangelize the world, beginning in your own neighborhood and working outward into the uttermost parts of the earth.

If the power of God is conspicuously absent in your life, the first thing you might want to ask yourself is this: "Is my life turned outward? Am I concerned about other people? Do I use my life's resources of time and money to get people saved or to influence this world for God in a way that will prepare them for salvation?"

Ask yourself those questions. Regardless of the call of God on our lives, we all share this mandate. If that is not the way you see life, then you have another agenda, and that is why the power is not going to operate.

Satan's Strategy of Distraction

One of the enemy's principle reasons for bringing sickness and infirmity, poverty and lack and oppression of every sort to the body of Christ is to get our focus turned inward. If he can get us to feel sorry for ourselves, then we will no longer use our resources to lead people to the Lord and the power of God will never flow in our lives. In that case, we will cease to be a threat to him.

Do not let Satan focus your attention inward; it will cost you the power. The most natural, carnal thing is for us to be concerned about ourselves and to make ourselves seem to be compassionate and concerned about the lost but not really mean it.

In that condition, we do not have our hearts aligned with the purpose of God. We need to use all of our resources to get people in church, get them saved, get them grown up on the Word and get the gospel preached to all of the world. We are still too focused on our own concerns.

What hangs in the balance is the power of God working in your life. You can ask God to show you how your light can shine. "Lord, how can I use my collection of abilities and gifts for Your purpose? How can I best be used by You to be influential for the gospel?"

He will show you, but it will never work properly until you have aligned your life's purpose with His. Then His power will flow in and through your life. You will find your needs getting met. You will find provision being made for you. You will find life more exciting than it has ever been.

Instead of being oppressed about what you do not have, you will be excited about what God is doing, not only in you, but through you. You will see lives being changed because you are obeying His Word. Things *will* be radically different.

CHAPTER 19 NINETEEN

The Seventh Seal

Now we come to the seventh and final seal:

> When He opened the seventh seal, there was silence in heaven for about half an hour. And I saw the seven angels who stand before God, and to them were given seven trumpets. Then another angel, having a golden censer, came and stood at the altar. He was given much incense, that he should offer it with the prayers of all the saints upon the golden altar which was before the throne.
>
> And the smoke of the incense, with the prayers of the saints, ascended before God from the angel's hand. Then the angel took the censer, filled it with fire from the altar, and threw it to the earth. And there were noises, thunderings, lightnings, and an earthquake.
>
> So the seven angels who had the seven trumpets prepared themselves to sound.

The first angel sounded: And hail and fire followed, mingled with blood, and they were thrown to the earth. And a third of the trees were burned up, and all green grass was burned up.

Then the second angel sounded: And something like a great mountain burning with fire was thrown into the sea, and a third of the sea became blood. And a third of the living creatures in the sea died, and a third of the ships were destroyed.

Revelation 8:1-9

Remember, the apostle John was seeing things in a vision for which he had no words. But today, we are blessed with a technological society which has access to vast amounts of information not available to people of John's day.

What Is Happening Here?

My personal opinion, and it is shared by several commentators, is that a meteor storm will produce the effects the apostle John is trying to describe here. Meteorites are space debris which enter our atmosphere at very high rates of speed, many thousands of miles an hour. When they hit our atmosphere, the friction generates such an intense heat that they begin to incinerate and burn up. That is what a shooting star is.

Now, a meteor storm is an astronomical phenomenon which happens when our planet encounters a large amount of debris as it moves through space. A meteor shower puts on a real fireworks show in the sky.

Now, the meteorites in this chapter of Revelation are large enough that they are not burned up in space; they actually hit the earth. **Hail and fire followed, mingled with blood** (v. 7). What hits the earth is a little burning meteorite about the size of a marble. It resembles hail, but yet it is hot and fiery red like blood.

John also says they cause trees and grass to burn. They will be so hot they will literally set part of the geography on fire where they strike.

A Whole Mountain

I believe when John describes **something like a great mountain burning with fire...thrown into the sea** (v. 8), he is seeing a huge meteorite strike the earth.

Many Bible prophecy authorities feel the outpouring of God's judgment and wrath is going to be centered around the geographical region of the old Roman Empire—an area comprised principally of Europe, parts of the Middle East, North Africa and up into the British Isles and Scandinavia—because that will be the Antichrist's headquarters.

Some scholars even suggest that only that area of the world where the Antichrist has direct domain and rule will experience the Tribulation.

That, in my opinion, is inconsistent with the whole context of Scripture, however. The whole world is going to be in tribulation, no doubt about it. The first five seals demonstrate that there will be great heartache, pain, suffering and tribulation across the whole earth. Nevertheless, the focal point will undoubtedly be that part of the world.

I believe the sea mentioned here is most likely the Mediterranean, as it will be within the boundaries of the Antichrist's empire.

A Burning Star

Then the third angel sounded: and a great star fell from heaven, burning like a torch, and it fell on a third of the rivers and on the springs of water; and the name of the star is Wormwood; and a third of the waters became wormwood; and many men died from the water, because it was made bitter.

Revelation 8:10,11

Here we have another meteorite, I believe. **A great star...from heaven, burning like a torch** is a pretty good description of a meteorite for a man who does not know what he is seeing in natural terms. This one, instead of falling in the oceans, will fall on a third of the rivers and the springs of waters, the sources of those rivers. God is referring to the waters which support and are so basic to our human existence.

Interestingly, virtually every river in Europe has its origin in the Alps. If this meteorite were to land in the Alps, then indeed it would poison the fountains of waters, or the sources of these rivers.

One-Third, One-Third and One-Third

Then the fourth angel sounded: And a third of the sun was struck, a third of the moon, and a third of the stars, so that a third of them were darkened. A third of the day did not shine, and likewise the night.

Revelation 8:12

It is obvious to me that John is not saying we will lose a third of the sun, moon or stars. He is talking about the *light* they shed on the earth. The natural available light will be reduced by a third. This progression is consistent with the previous three trumpets we read about.

A huge meteorite impacting earth would raise tremendous clouds of dust. You have heard about this phenomenon in regard to a nuclear holocaust; the term *nuclear winter* refers to the devastating effect on life that a nuclear bomb blast would cause, lifting vast quantities of dust and debris into our atmosphere.

A nuclear holocaust would produce a cloud which would engulf the globe, limiting the sunlight, lowering the temperature and totally changing life on the planet. It has been proven scientifically that a large meteorite striking the earth would have the same effect.

So a meteor storm will be followed by two major meteorite impacts. To me it seems reasonable to assume that huge clouds of dust and debris will have blown into the atmosphere and begun to block out the light from the sun, the moon and the stars.

The sky will be so darkened that the sun will have to be almost directly overhead for there to be normal daylight. The day's light would be shortened by a third; dawn would come later and sunset earlier.

What Is the Plan?

You ask, "What could the purpose of all this be? It does not seem to be all that devastating. If God is trying to stop the Antichrist and his dealings on earth, all this meteorite stuff does not seem to be the most efficient way to go about it."

I think it is. We saw the six seals listed in Matthew 24, and Jesus adds this in verse 22: **"And unless those days were shortened, no flesh would be saved; but for the elect's sake those days will be shortened."** Now, we know He is not talking about shortening the three-and-a-half years which remain of the Tribulation; that is a set time. No, this is a literal reference to the shortening of the daylight hours so the believers have the obscurity of darkness to flee their persecutors, the forces of the Antichrist.

In God's unfolding plan, this is probably part of the purpose for the shroud of darkness.

The Prayers of the Saints

Then another angel, having a golden censer, came and stood at the altar. He was given much incense, that he should offer it with the prayers of all the saints upon the golden altar which was before the throne.

And the smoke of the incense, with the prayers of the saints, ascended before God from the angel's hand. Then the angel took the censer, filled it with fire from the altar, and threw it to the earth. And there were noises, thunderings, lightnings, and an earthquake.

Revelation 8:3-5

It is the prayers of the saints—your prayers—which launch the seven trumpet judgments.

Now when He had taken the scroll, the four living creatures and the twenty-four elders fell down before the Lamb,

each having a harp, and golden bowls full of incense, which are the prayers of the saints.

Then one of the four living creatures gave to the seven angels seven golden bowls full of the wrath of God who lives forever and ever.

Revelation 5:8; 15:7

These are the same golden bowls which were full of incense, but here they are full of the wrath of God.

In one place they are described as holding the prayers of the saints. Once those prayers have ascended to God as burning incense, then they hold the wrath of God. We just saw in chapter 8 that the prayers of the saints initiated the seven trumpet judgments.

What Your Prayers Really Do

Most Christians do not really know what their prayers do, if they believe they do anything at all. Most think, *I am asking God about something I need, but about half the time there does not seem to be an answer. Who knows why?*

The Word makes it clear that when prayer is properly offered, it is always answered. Always. This means you have to pray properly—the way the Bible says to pray. You cannot just throw any old kind of prayer up to God and expect to get results. But the right kind of prayer, based on the Word and offered with the right attitude, will always get results!

"So, how do I do that?" you ask.

There are six keys to praying so you will get results:

1   You must pray in line with God's Word.

2.   You must believe the Word you pray.

3.   You cannot have any unforgiveness against anyone.

4.   Your prayer cannot be motivated by selfish desire.

5.   Your prayer must be fervent.

6.   You must pray in the Spirit as well.

If you will pray in this way, you will be praying in accordance with biblical principles and every prayer will produce a result. God's Word will not return to Him void; it will accomplish what He sends it to do. (Isa. 55:11.) Every time you pray, there is a result, and the result is either blessing or judgment.

When you pray and petition God for something, 99 percent of the time God fulfills that prayer in your life through another person. When you pray for prosperity, it is unlikely that God will drop a sack of money from heaven on your head. He could; He is God. But His purpose is to use humanity. If you need to receive a blessing, there is somebody else who needs to give a blessing.

God works through people who are yielded to Him. But when the will of man refuses the leadership of the Lord, when disobedience occurs, what happens then? Judgment.

Just as God works through people, so does the devil. The devil cannot perpetrate evil directly on you. He has to work through somebody who is either consciously or unconsciously yielded to him.

God's Word is not going to return to Him void. When you pray, He is going to respond and begin working on people to accomplish what you pray for. When they are obedient, blessing flows to you *and* to them.

But when they disobey, judgment is accruing. God is not a vindictive God; but He is a just God, and the books are going to be balanced. That judgment is not necessarily going to come on the disobedient individual right at that point. God often waits, because He is a merciful God. He would prefer for that person to repent so He could show His great mercy.

But if that person will not repent, God must execute judgment. That is what the golden bowls are about. That's why their contents turn from prayers into judgment. These prayers have been stored up, holding back judgment which has never been poured out on man for his disobedience. They are a big part of what is going to occur during the Tribulation period.

There have been a lot of seeds sown by saints of God down through the centuries which, for a variety of reasons, have not been reaped. But the seed is incorruptible. What is the seed? It is the Word of God.

Many saints of old who gave their lives in service to God did not know they had a right to a harvest and never exercised their faith for it. They did not collect it. Or evil men got in the way and, because they did not know the authority they had in the name of Jesus, the enemy was able to steal their answer.

Does that mean the seed is gone forever? No. Remember, the seed is incorruptible, and God is not mocked: Every seed which has been sown will produce a harvest. For generations there has been seed sown which has not yet produced. At the end of this age, there will be a great harvest.

So when you pray properly, your prayer is going to promote the plan of God, either as a blessing or as a judgment. Do not think your prayer is getting no response. Do not think you are wasting your time. Do you know what you are doing? You are fulfilling the primary responsibility of your relationship with God.

Prayer is to be a major aspect of our walks with God, because it is only as His Word returns to Him through prayer that it can produce what He desires in the earth.

CHAPTER TWENTY

Godly Sorrow

Revelation 8 and 9 chronicle the events transpiring on the earth during the Tribulation. The first four trumpet judgments have to do with various astronomical and geological events, and the last three trumpets are judgments specifically directed at humanity.

> **"Woe, woe, woe to the inhabitants of the earth because of the three remaining blasts of the trumpet of the three angels who are about to sound!"**
>
> **Revelation 8:13**

These are called the *woe* judgments.

Chapter 9 begins the first of these woe judgments with the fifth angel.

> **Then the fifth angel sounded: and I saw a star fallen from heaven to the earth. To him was given the key to the bottomless pit.**
>
> **Revelation 9:1**

Several commentators and teachers have tried to determine who the star is; they attempt to turn the star into a person or entity. There really is no basis for doing that.

Because the previous chapter relates astronomical phenomena, there is no reason to think the context has changed when the fifth trumpet sounds. Indeed, it is logical to conclude that it is a literal falling star. **To him** refers not to the star, but to the angel who will sound the trumpet. He will be given the key to the bottomless pit.

Who holds the keys to hell and death? Jesus does. Jesus will give the key to the bottomless pit to the angel who will sound the trumpet.

The Bottomless Pit Opened

And he opened the bottomless pit, and smoke arose out of the pit like the smoke of a great furnace. So the sun and the air were darkened because of the smoke of the pit.

Revelation 9:2

This could be a volcano or an eruption occurring as a result of the impact of the falling star, which will have occurred when the fifth angel has sounded his trumpet.

But when the pit is opened, all hell will break loose—literally.

Then out of the smoke locusts came upon the earth. And to them was given power, as the scorpions of the earth have power. They were commanded not to harm the grass of the earth, or any green thing, or any tree, but only those men who do not have the seal of God on their foreheads. And they were not given authority to kill them, but to torment them for five months. Their torment was like the torment of a scorpion when it strikes a man. In those days men will seek death and will not find it; they will desire to die, and death will flee from them.

Revelation 9:3-6

There are differing opinions about the locusts. Is this a literal insect infestation? Are the locusts symbolic?

Or is this perhaps a spiritual manifestation we are dealing with? I believe so. I believe the locusts refer to a demonic manifestation. Verse 11 says, **And they had as king over them the angel of the bottomless pit, whose name in Hebrew is Abaddon, but in Greek he has the name Apollyon.**

Abaddon is an overlord with tremendous power in the kingdom of darkness. His name literally means "destruction."[1] He shows up in the Word earlier as the death angel who takes the firstborn of the Egyptians. This is the high power in the kingdom of darkness.

Revelation 9:11 says Abaddon is the king over them. He is not king over a swarm of insects; he is king over a demonic horde. So, it seems apparent that the locusts are a reference to a releasing of a demon horde from the bottomless pit.

Where Did They Come From?

This raises some interesting questions. We know that demonic activity goes on in the earth right now and that all the demons, Satan included, are not locked up in the bottomless pit right now. So who is being loosed from the bottomless pit?

Well, let me remind you that not all of the angels who rebelled with Satan were given freedom to join him. A portion of the angelic host were chained in everlasting darkness until the Day of Judgment.

Jude 1:6 gives us a little more insight:

> **And the angels who did not keep their proper domain,
> but left their own abode, He has reserved in everlasting
> chains under darkness for the judgment of the great day.**

I believe this horde is the angels referred to in Genesis as the **sons of God** (a term commonly used in the Bible for angels) who, prior to the Flood, cohabited with human women, **daughters of men,** and produced a race of giants. (Gen. 6:4.)

This, to me, is what Jude meant when he said they **left their own abode.** They left the spiritual realm and attempted to live in the natural realm, the proper abode of humans, and actually produced an offspring of giants we see referred to throughout the Old Testament. Remember the giants of Canaan, the Promised Land? Remember Goliath?

Now, the reason Satan did this was that God had spoken to the serpent and told him, "The seed of woman is going to crush the head of the serpent." (Gen. 3:15.) Satan was making an effort to poison the seed of man so Jesus, the "Seed of the woman," would not be able to come through the seed of man.

It was Satan's intent to genetically predispose man to evil. But God will protect our freedom to choose at all costs; He never forces Himself on us, and He is not going to allow the enemy to force his evil on mankind either. That is why he had the children of Israel, under Moses and Joshua, attack the giants who were the demons' offspring.

Bad to the Bone

This horde of evil angels will be released from the pit when the fifth angel opens the bottomless pit. We have not seen the really bad demons yet. The demons we deal with on a daily basis are Boy Scouts compared to the ones released in the Tribulation.

They are referred to as locusts, and they are commanded not to hurt any vegetation on earth. They can harm only the men who do not have the seal of God on them.

They are commanded not to kill them but only torment them. Who are the ones with the seal of God? The 144,000 Jewish evangelists.

To understand the operation of these particular demons, we need to understand the effect of a scorpion sting on a human being. This is the type of torment they will inflict on mankind.

We think of scorpions as little things, with a sting not much different than the sting of a bee. But in the area of the world where this was written, and especially on the isle of Patmos where John was, scorpions are five to six times larger than the ones in North America. Their sting is incredibly painful, causing all sorts of sickness and fever, and very often the sting is fatal.

This demonic activity will not be allowed to produce death but rather will cause the same kind of torment that scorpion poison produces in the human body.

A scorpion's poison is completely different from almost every other venomous insect's or reptile's. For instance, snake venom attacks either the cardiovascular system or the central nervous system and produces paralysis or death through those systems.

But the poison of a scorpion goes straight to the brain stem and, in large enough doses, ultimately produces dementia. But not all at once; it is a gradual process of worsening mental torment until the individual goes out of his or her mind.

That is what the scorpion sting does if it is not properly treated and is allowed to have its full range of effect. And that is the effect these demons will have on humankind. Humans are going to be tormented mentally to a degree that we cannot even imagine. They are going to want to die but will be unable to.

Like an Army of Locusts

John describes what these demons looked like to him.

The shape of the locusts was like horses prepared for battle. On their heads were crowns of something like gold, and their faces were like the faces of men. They had hair like women's hair, and their teeth were like lions' teeth. And they had breastplates of iron, and the sound of their wings was like the sound of chariots with many horses running into battle. They had tails like scorpions, and there were stings in their tails. Their power was to hurt men five months.

Revelation 9:7-10

Let me remind you that John was seeing in the Spirit. Also, John did not really know what he was looking at. He did not have proper words for what he saw, but he came up with the word *locusts* and went from there.

The men who are attacked by this demonic horde will not see them any more than you do when you experience a demonic influence in your life. You only experience the *effect* of the attack.

The people in that day will not see these creatures John describes; they will simply become tormented mentally. Their mental condition will deteriorate to the point that many will become completely insane. They will want to die, but they will be unable to and will not know why. This will go on for a period of five months.

The Woe of the Sixth Trumpet

One woe is past. Behold, still two more woes are coming after these things:

> **Then the sixth angel sounded: And I heard a voice from the four horns of the golden altar which is before God, saying to the sixth angel who had the trumpet, "Release the four angels who are bound at the great river Euphrates." So the four angels, who had been prepared for the hour and day and month and year, were released to kill a third of mankind. Now the number of the army of the horsemen was two hundred million; and I heard the number of them.**
>
> **Revelation 9:13-16**

Is this a spiritual army or a literal one? I believe it is a literal army.

Most of the commentaries which take the position that this is a spiritual army were written back in the 1940s. These commentators believed, based on the world's population at the time, that it was impossible for any nation or combination of nations to raise a 200 million-man army.

But since the 1940s, the earth's population has increased fivefold and, in the latter part of the 1970s, the president of China reported to the world that he now had a standing army of over 200 million men!

200 Million Strong

I want you to see that it is not coincidental that the Chinese have a 200 million-man army.

Then the sixth angel poured out his bowl on the great river Euphrates, and its water was dried up, so that the way of the kings from the east might be prepared.

Revelation 16:12

The kings from the east is a reference to China. What do they need to be prepared for? Armaggedon. The end of the Jewish dispensation comes with the battle of Armageddon, and that battle is comprised of two armies who oppose the army of the Lord.

The Antichrist will lead his army out of the geographical area of the Roman Empire and will move south toward the plains of Megiddo in Israel. Then this 200 million-man army will move up from the southeast toward that same plain to meet Christ and His army at the Battle of Armageddon.

But before this can occur, a great natural barrier has to be overcome. In order for a 200 million-man army to make it to the plains of Israel, somehow a great river barrier must be removed.

The Euphrates River is not a little river. You might think that with today's modern, mechanized armies certainly a river crossing would not be a big deal. The problem is that the river Euphrates is 1600 miles long, 400 yards wide, and 30 feet deep on average. You cannot just drive across it.

Imagine trying to get 200 million men across the Mississippi River. To move an army of that size, with all of their attendant equipment, would take longer than the time left before the Battle of Armageddon is to occur.

So something has to be done about this natural barrier. The sixth angel in chapter 16 pours out his vial on the river as part of the vial judgments and supernaturally dries up the river to prepare the way of the kings of the east.

Then we read in Revelation 9:14 that when the sixth angel sounds his trumpet, four angels who are bound in the great river Euphrates are now loosed.

I agree with the viewpoint which says that the release of these four angels is a spiritual loosing for this army of 200 million men to begin mobilizing and moving toward their point of final confrontation.

Apparently there will have been spiritual restraints on this great army. China has had over 200 million men in arms for two decades now and has not done anything with them. I believe they have been under a spiritual restraint; and when these four angels are loosed, they will release the spiritual restraints which will have held back this army until that time.

West to War

With the restraints removed, the army will begin mobilizing and moving toward their most natural enemies: India, Pakistan and Afghanistan—the nations standing between them and the river Euphrates. These peoples have historically been China's natural enemies; there are border skirmishes among them all the time.

What has kept the giant China from simply absorbing her neighbors? There has been a spiritual restraint in place. The four angels will release the restraint, and then the army will begin moving toward the Euphrates, toward their moment of destiny when they will meet Christ at Armageddon. But on the way, the Word says they will slay a third of mankind.

It is not a coincidence that India, Pakistan and Afghanistan alone are home to more than one-third of the world's population. Considerably more, actually.

I believe there is going to be great carnage as the 200 million-man army out of China destroys their natural enemies in their move toward the Euphrates River, which, by chapter 16, will be dried up. They will cross and head toward their ultimate defeat on the plains of Armageddon.

This view fits well both with the context of Scripture and with current events.

What Is That?

John's description of that army, beginning in Revelation 9:17, is almost humorous to me. I can just imagine somebody living almost 2000 years ago trying to describe modern, mechanized warfare.

How would you have described a tank or an armored personnel carrier or a mobile rocket launcher if you had been in John's shoes? They would look alive to you because they move; and with their cannons and guns, they would look like huge monsters of some sort with fire belching out of them.

As we read this description, it is clear this is what is happening to poor John. He is trying to describe modern mechanized warfare, something not even conceivable to a man of his day.

And thus I saw the horses in the vision: those who sat on them had breastplates of fiery red, hyacinth blue, and sulfur yellow; and the heads of the horses were like the heads of lions; and out of their mouths came fire, smoke, and brimstone. By these three plagues a third of mankind was killed—by the fire and the smoke and the brimstone which came out of their mouths. For their power is in their mouth and in their tails; for their tails are like serpents, having heads; and with them they do harm.

Revelation 9:17-19

A tank's turret can turn all the way around. It can be shooting backward or forward, depending on the way it is moving over the terrain. John is saying, "Fire and brimstone is flying out of its head and tail." He is describing a modern tank without knowing what he is looking at.

And Yet...

The most astounding thing about this chapter to me is found in the last two verses:

But the rest of mankind, who were not killed by these plagues, did not repent of the works of their hands, that they should not worship demons, and idols of gold, silver, brass, stone, and wood, which can neither see nor hear nor walk; and they did not repent of their murders or their sorceries or their sexual immorality or their thefts.

Revelation 9:20,21

Is it not amazing that humanity can experience what they will be experiencing here and still not turn to God to repent of the things which brought this on them?

When I first read through this passage, that stuck out like a sore thumb. *How in the world could they not repent? Are they nuts?* I thought. *They see the greatest outpouring of God's judgment the world has ever seen, but they do not repent? How can that be?*

The Holy Spirit immediately said to my heart, *It has always been that way.* And I suddenly realized that even in my experience in ministry, when I have seen God do amazing things to bring healing or ministry to people's lives, they still do not change their ways.

Why do some people keep plodding down the same path when they know better? Why do they remain unchanged when the results of their choices harm their lives and bring pain and cursing upon them? Why do they continue in sin when they see the negative consequences?

Some people simply will not turn around, no matter what. I am not talking about unbelievers, but Christians—Christians who basically decide to live a little bit in line with the Word and a little bit in line with the world. It is not possible to do that permanently. You will eventually wind up completely on one side or the other.

Godly Sorrow

I want you to understand the importance of repentance and how it works in your life.

What produces repentance? What causes somebody to repent?

For godly sorrow produces repentance leading to salvation, not to be regretted; but the sorrow of the world produces death.

2 Corinthians 7:10

To *repent* implies a reversal of direction.[2] It does not mean to cover yourself with sackcloth and ashes. It does not mean to grovel in the dirt before the altar.

Godly sorrow produces repentance leading to salvation. In other words, a change is made that enables God's purpose to be realized in your life.

The word *salvation* in this verse is not just a reference to our eternal destiny in heaven. *Salvation* here can be translated "health."[3] It means preservation or protection.

The phrase **not to be regretted** in this verse tells us that you do not just do this for a week and then go back to your old ways. That happens a lot. Somebody will say, "I have to change," and he does for a week or two; but then he goes right back to his old ways. That is failed willpower, not repentance.

But godly sorrow will cause repentance which will not be reversed, but will produce the salvation of God—the deliverance, healing, preservation and provision of God.

The second half of the verse adds to our understanding: **...but the sorrow of the world produces death.** So we have two kinds of sorrow: One takes you to the blessing and the salvation of God; the other takes you to death.

A Permanent Change

For observe this very thing, that you sorrowed in a godly manner: What diligence it produced in you, what clearing of yourselves, what indignation, what fear, what vehement desire, what zeal, what vindication! In all things you proved yourselves to be clear in this matter.

2 Corinthians 7:11

The repentance produced by godly sorrow changes a person. It takes a lethargic Christian—somebody who has been marginal in the kingdom of God—and produces a great zeal and vehement desire to do God's will and a righteous indignation at the touch of evil. It changes the way that person lives. It changes the way that person talks.

Worldly sorrow, however, takes you the other direction. It produces a progression leading to death. We are either moving toward life or moving toward death. There is no in-between. The Lord put it this way: **"I call heaven and earth as witnesses today against you, that I have set before you**

life and death, blessing and cursing; therefore choose life, that both you and your descendants may live" (Deut. 30:19).

The will of the Father is for you to choose life and blessing, but it is your choice. And that choice is before you each day. Life and blessing, or death and cursing; the choice is yours.

Since sorrow is a progressive event, you will begin moving in one direction or the other, and the way you are going will manifest what is in your life—blessings or cursings.

The slide toward death is always evidenced by the operation of the curse in our lives. God is not in the cursing business; He is in the blessing business. So as we move toward life, blessing is our primary indicator. These are the primary road signs on the highways of life and death: blessing and cursing.

Do you want to know what I mean when I say *cursing?* Read Deuteronomy 28:16-68. It covers just about everything you could possibly think of and more—everything from wayward kids to unfaithful spouses to every sickness and disease known to humanity to complete loss of financial security. All of that is under the curse.

If you are born again, you have been redeemed from all of it, because Jesus has redeemed us from the curse. (Gal. 3:13.) But 2 Corinthians 7:10-11 tells us that if we are walking on the wrong path, then sorrow will indicate to us that we are going the wrong way. If sorrow comes to you, it should be a flag. "Something is wrong here. I am out of the will of God. I have made a mistake. I am off the path."

The Word says the blessing of the Lord brings no sorrow with it. (Prov. 10:22.) So when sorrow comes, you know something is wrong. Here is a key point: Your sorrow is neither godly nor worldly. Whether it works repentance leading to salvation or takes you to death depends entirely on what you do with it.

The World's Sorrow

When are people in the world sorry? When they get caught. When they lose something, such as money or a relationship or a possession. It is all turned inward. There is another word for worldly sorrow: *self-pity.* "I do not deserve this! Why did God let this happen to me? I have done everything I know to do. I just feel so bad. I am so unhappy."

When we begin feeling sorry for ourselves, it leads us onto the road toward death, because that is the sorrow of the world.

On the other hand, if we have godly sorrow, change will come. Repentance will lead to salvation so we can experience the will of God, and it will light our fire, putting the desire for the things of God inside us.

Godly Sorrow

So what is godly sorrow? The Word defines it for us in Romans 2:4:

Or do you despise the riches of His goodness, forbearance, and longsuffering, not knowing that the goodness of God leads you to repentance?

In other words, do not despise the goodness of God, but be conscious and aware of His goodness. Then when you feel that sorrow because you have moved off the road of His perfect will, the sorrow is not oriented toward self-pity but toward God's goodness and how you have despised it.

That is what causes a genuine turnaround.

If you decide to change because you get caught, you will do it again. But if you realize God has extended His grace to you time and time again and has been good to you with every opportunity He had, that produces a thankful heart. Then when sorrow comes, you will grieve for having let God down—not because you did not get what you wanted.

This is why an attitude of thanksgiving toward God is so important. It keeps you oriented toward His goodness. The enemy's strategy is to make you look at what you do not have so when something goes wrong, you fall into self-pity and worldly sorrow, which lead to death.

But if you are looking at the goodness of God—at how He has blessed you—then when you see you have failed, your sorrow is that you have not measured up to His standard of goodness.

The danger is that some will become so self-centered that even in the outpouring of the worst judgment this earth will ever see, they still will not repent. All they will do is talk about how bad it is and say, "Woe is me." But the lesson in this for us is that we can turn sorrow into a godly thing now, and it will profit us greatly.

CHAPTER TWENTY-ONE

Mysteries

Revelation 10 provides a glimpse of other things happening at the same time as the trumpet judgments.

> **I saw still another mighty angel coming down from heaven, clothed with a cloud. And a rainbow was on his head, his face was like the sun, and his feet like pillars of fire. He had a little book open in his hand. And he set his right foot on the sea and his left foot on the land, and cried with a loud voice, as when a lion roars. When he cried out, seven thunders uttered their voices. Now when the seven thunders uttered their voices, I was about to write; but I heard a voice from heaven saying to me, "Seal up the things which the seven thunders uttered, and do not write them."**

> **Revelation 10:1-4**

It is fruitless to speculate about what the seven thunders are. God said to seal them up, and we are simply not going to figure out what they are, no matter how clever we think we are.

There is also some debate over who this mighty angel is, but to me, it is very clearly an appearance of the Lord Jesus Christ. He is referred to on numerous occasions in the Word as the Angel of the Lord, as a captain of the Lord's host. Remember *angel* simply means messenger.[1] The description is also reminiscent of Revelation 1 when John saw Jesus. Furthermore, He had a little book opened in His hand, and earlier we saw that Jesus will be the only one found worthy to open the book.

Also, when this mighty angel speaks, it is as a lion roaring. Jesus is called the Lion of the tribe of Judah.

Perhaps the most significant indicator to me that this is Jesus is in chapter 11: **"And I will give power to my two witnesses..."** (v. 3).

Of whom are the witnesses going to testify? Jesus. I believe this could not be one of the heavenly beings called angels; this is an appearance of Jesus Himself.

The Mystery Is Finished

The angel whom I saw standing on the sea and on the land raised up his hand to heaven and swore by Him who lives forever and ever, who created heaven and the things that are in it, the earth and the things that are in it, and the sea and the things that are in it, that there should be delay no longer, but in the days of the sounding of the seventh angel, when he is about to sound, the mystery of God would be finished, as He declared to His servants the prophets.

Revelation 10:5-7

The **mystery of God** [will] **be finished!** That is an important statement many have used to predict a mid-Tribulation Rapture because the church age is referred to as the mystery.

Now, if the mystery of God is going to be finished at the seventh trumpet, which comes at the three-and-a-half-year point of the Tribulation, then the church is, indeed, going to be here for the first half of the Tribulation.

But that could not be accurate, because the mystery referred to here which is going to be finished has been declared to His servants, the prophets. Yet we know the prophets never saw the church age.

You have to understand, the church age is a *part* of the mystery but not the whole thing. The part of the mystery remaining to be finished is the part which was declared to His servants, the prophets.

And that He may send Jesus Christ, who was preached to you before, whom heaven must receive until the times of restoration of all things, which God has spoken by the mouth of all His holy prophets since the world began.

Acts 3:20,21

The times of the restoration of all things is the Millennium, because Jesus is not coming back to this earth until His Second Advent. So until then, heaven must receive Him. We see what the prophets saw—His Second Advent.

Eat the Book

Then the voice which I heard from heaven spoke to me again and said, "Go, take the little book which is open in the hand of the angel who stands on the sea and on the earth."

So I went to the angel and said to him, "Give me the little book."

And he said to me, "Take and eat it; and it will make your stomach bitter, but it will be as sweet as honey in your mouth."

Then I took the little book out of the angel's hand and ate it, and it was as sweet as honey in my mouth. But when I had eaten it, my stomach became bitter.

Revelation 10:8-10

John is given a revelation of something called **the seven thunders.** We are not told what they are, because the Lord said to seal them up. That sealing puts them in a Bible classification of being a "mystery." When something is sealed to human understanding, it is a mystery. We see that this mystery will come to an end when the seventh angel sounds his trumpet.

Then God told John to take the little book, which is a revelation of the seven thunders, the things John had to seal up and not write, and He said, **"Eat it."**

Now, that does not mean John literally ate a book. The term *eat* here is a metaphor for absorbing the contents.[2] You have probably heard someone say, "I have been feeding on the Word." You knew they did not mean they had actually taken bites out of their Bibles; they meant, "I'm absorbing the contents."

When John "eats" the book, it tastes like honey; but then it becomes bitter in his stomach. Likewise, when a mystery is revealed to you, it is exciting. There are few things that can stir the human heart any more than when you have received a revelation from God.

Unfortunately, many people have never experienced this, but when you know God has shown you something about His plan for your life, that is exciting! And it is sweet. But then a few days later, after slugging it out at the office and remaining in the same old status quo, this great and grand thing God has shown you, which was sweet when you received it, becomes a little bitter. You realize you are still in your present circumstances, and you are not quite sure that what you have seen is going to come to pass.

So it was with John. Seeing the end of things and the revelation of the mystery must have been very sweet. But some of the things he saw involved judgment too, and that had to carry an edge—a little bitterness—with it.

Understanding Mysteries

I want to spend a little more time on the subject of mysteries because without an understanding of *what* a spiritual mystery is, *how* to unravel it and *how* to move into it, you can never fully experience God's highest will for your life.

To move into the destiny God has prepared for you, you must choose to align your life with His plan. This means you have to first discern His plan. Yet much of the Bible is a mystery.

The word *mystery* in the Greek simply means "secret, or hidden from human understanding."[3] A mystery is not something you would ever think about or consider, and your intellect is not fruitful when you do.

Because so much of the plan of God is characterized as a mystery, we must learn how to unravel these mysteries if we want to understand how to move down the path toward fulfilling His will.

The Mystery of the Kingdom

We see this word *mystery* used in a number of different areas. There are different types of mysteries in the Bible. One primary spiritual mystery, for instance, is the kingdom of God to those who are outside of it. (Mark 4:11.) To the unbeliever, the kingdom of God is a mystery. Everything about it—the Bible, heaven and hell, God and the devil—is all a mystery.

Many self-proclaimed intellectuals have read a lot of the Bible and may even be able to quote reams of Scripture, but they are still in the dark about it. As unsaved men and women, they are still outside looking in at things they cannot understand.

That is why it's important not to argue with an unbeliever about the things of God. Do not debate the Scripture. You will never get anywhere, because unbelievers cannot penetrate the mystery until they become a part of the kingdom.

How do they do that? Jesus said they have to repent of their sins and be converted. They need to hear about Jesus. That is the only relevant issue to people who are outside the kingdom of God. Until they receive Him by faith, the Bible will never be open to them. But once they do, they will begin to see things they could never see before.

The Mystery of the Church Age

Beyond the nature of the kingdom of God, another mystery is the church age. It is a lesser mystery, contained within the greater mystery of God's kingdom. It was a mystery to all of the Old Testament saints and prophets. It was never prophesied or foreshadowed in the Old Testament.

Now, within the church age, there are many other mysteries. For instance, Colossians 1:27 says:

> **To them God willed to make known what are the riches of the glory of this mystery among the Gentiles: which is Christ in you, the hope of glory.**

This means that when you are born again, you become a temple of the Holy Spirit. You become the dwelling place of the living God. No more is He removed by a great gulf impossible to bridge. He lives in you. This is a life-changing revelation. But, unfortunately, it remains a mystery, not a reality, to most Christians.

For most Christians, it is still a mystery that the Creator of the universe lives inside of them. If it were not a mystery to them, they would not be so oppressed by their circumstances. If it were not a mystery, they would not be taking God into the bar or to parties with them.

The Mystery of Marriage

> **For this reason a man shall leave his father and mother and be joined to his wife, and the two shall become one flesh." This is a great mystery, but I speak concerning Christ and the church.**
>
> **Ephesians 5:31,32**

The Bible calls marriage a mystery comparable to the mystery of Christ and His church. If you can understand one, you can understand the other. Unfortunately, in modern America we do not often understand either.

Believers struggle to know why they cannot get in right relationship with the Lord. They wonder why they hear others talking about their experiences with God yet never have any themselves. Meanwhile, their marriages are falling apart. But they never make the connection.

Mysteries

Paul said the mystery of marriage is like the mystery of Christ and His church.

For a moment, think about the creative intent of God in Genesis. He created Adam, complete and entire. There was no woman initially. All of the components needed for human existence were complete in one body of flesh called Adam. Everything about mankind was included in that one body.

Later on, God decided Adam needed a suitable helper. Did He just go gather up some more dust and make Eve? No. He took Eve from Adam— and not just physically; all of the components of personality that make a woman a woman were extracted from the being called Adam. (A careful study of the Hebrew words in Genesis will confirm this remarkable truth.)

The significance of this is that the *one flesh* condition of mankind was present before Eve was taken out of Adam. *That* was the creation which was made in the image and likeness of God. *That* was the creation given dominion over this earth and everything in it.

Before you were married, if you were a believer, you had a one-flesh relationship with Christ as your husband. (It does not matter if you are male or female here, because we are all the bride of Christ). However, when you were married you joined yourself to another human being in a one-flesh relationship. Now the degree of dominion and authority you walk in, the degree of the power of God flowing in your life and the degree to which you become like Christ are connected to the degree to which you become one flesh with your spouse. Remember, faith works by love.

The reverse is also true. Not only will your relationship with God, His effectiveness in using you and your ability to work the works of God increase as you become increasingly one flesh with your spouse; but as you become more like Jesus and "eat" the Word, your ability to be more one flesh with your spouse will increase dramatically.

When your life is not working right, the first place to look is at your marriage. Are you one flesh? What does being one flesh mean? It means to be so joined with one another in mind and in spirit that there is no gap at all between you. You are one complete entity, not merely two people who share a last name. This is an utter unreality for most marriages today.

Many husbands and wives say, "Well, that is just not possible! What kind of preaching is this?" This is the Bible, but it is still a mystery to them. The mystery would begin to unfold if they would relate to each other as the Bible says to.

The mystery would unfold, and they would come closer and closer, until they would eventually become one flesh. And great power and anointing would be released in their lives.

But a woman reads that she has to submit to her husband, and the first thing that comes to her mind is, *How in the world can I submit to that turkey?* Not every wife feels that way, but some do.

Or a husband looks at the Scripture which says he is to love his wife as his own body and thinks, *Well, she looked pretty good about thirty years ago, but now…*

We need to put aside "sophisticated," contemporary American thought about these things and get back to the Bible. It is the only way we will get a touch of the supernatural in our lives.

Unraveling the Mysteries

There are many other biblical mysteries, but space does not permit us to explore them all. The real question is, *How do we unravel them and align our lives with the will of God accordingly?*

The first thing you do is read the Word. That is where mysteries are revealed. Read it for yourself. Do not blindly accept what your church or any preacher—including this one—teaches without confirming it in the Word of God. You have to know that your understanding is lined up with the Word, but you will not know this unless you study the Word for yourself.

Secondly, you have to receive what you read. You cannot pick and choose what you want to accept because you like it. The only definition we have of Christianity is from the Bible. The only revelation we have of God is the Bible.

When you understand what the Word says and receive it by faith, then the light will go on and the Spirit of God will begin to bring illumination to the Word.

The Rapture will take on a whole different meaning. It will no longer be something weird or fanatical. Every time you think about it, a spark of excitement will flicker in your heart.

You will look at your marriage in an entirely different way. The mystery will begin to clear up when you receive the Word. You may not understand how treating your spouse a particular way will make much difference, but when you do it because you believe and receive the Word of God in your life, the mystery will be unveiled. Then your marriage can come to a place of truly being one flesh, and you will walk in power you could never walk in otherwise.

Unrevealed Mysteries

Well, what about the mysteries that are not revealed by the Bible? The Bible talks about other mysteries which are a major part of the plan of God, and yet they are never revealed or discussed any further in the Word. Why is that? There are two reasons.

One we see in 1 Corinthians 2:8, where Paul says that if Satan had known God's plan, he would not have crucified Jesus. So there are some things not addressed in the Word because the devil reads the Bible too. The Bible clearly teaches that Satan is a creature who is very interested in stopping the plan of God because its completion means his downfall. He is your adversary, and I can assure you that if he knows the plan of God for your life, he will put roadblocks up wherever he can.

Secondly, some mysteries are not revealed because the Bible is a revelation of God's general plan for all mankind. He could not put all the individual parts in here. He has a plan for your life; but the specifics are not in the Bible, so it is still a mystery. How is it revealed if the Word of God does not reveal it? God reveals it to us by His Spirit.

People may ask at this point, "Why is it not revealed to me? I still do not know what I am supposed to do."

Everything we receive from God we receive by faith. He will reveal mysteries to you if you will believe Him for it. Sit quietly before the Lord during the part of your day when you pray. Pray in the Spirit, and interpretation will begin to come. You will see things about God's plan for your life that you would never see any other way.

You will never unravel the mystery any other way than by sitting in the presence of God and praying in the Spirit, drawing with your faith on the ministry of the Holy Spirit to reveal God's plan to you. Only then will you begin to see these mysteries more clearly.

Absorbing the Revelation

John had to absorb the revelation. This means that when God brings *you* a revelation, you have to absorb it. You have to feed upon it. Whether it comes through the Word or the ministry of the Holy Spirit, if that mystery is going to be finished, you have to absorb it and take it into your heart by thinking about it, meditating on it and feeding on it until you have consumed it.

When God shows you something, if you do not go through this process, it will be no more than a "pizza dream" to you. You will have your prayer time and God will show you something great and grand, but two hours later you will end up writing it off as fantasy.

Once God reveals something to you, receive it by faith. Believe it just as strongly as you do the Word of God. Feed on it; meditate on it; think about it; see it coming to pass for your life.

Proclaiming the Mystery

Revelation 10:11 says,

And he said to me, "You must prophesy again about many peoples, nations, tongues, and kings."

This is a command to proclaim the Word of God and what you have seen by the Spirit when God shows you something and begins to unveil a mystery.

This does not mean you should talk about it to just anybody, however. Jesus called that "casting your pearls before swine." (Matt. 7:6.) You must not take the precious truths of God revealed to you by the Holy Spirit and plop them down before someone who will step on them or mock them or be a source of persecution in your life.

That is a big part of keeping the prince of this world from interfering with the plan of God for your life.

But in order for the mysteries to be finished, after you have absorbed the revelation sufficiently, the Spirit of God will move on you to proclaim it. You will make declarations by the Spirit about what God has shown you.

Very frequently, it will be prophetic preaching or teaching which actually does something in the Spirit to loose the plan of God, the mystery of God, to be finished in a particular area.

I believe these kinds of inspired proclamations, called prophecy here, are a prerequisite to the consummation of the mystery of God in your life. When you pray in the Spirit and He shows you a little bit about His plan for your life, the mystery begins to unravel.

You receive it by faith, you feed on it by meditating and thinking about it and letting it become bigger and more real to you, and then the day will come when the Spirit will move you to proclaim it. This will break things open in the spiritual realm, and these events will begin to come to pass.

CHAPTER TWENTY-TWO

The Two Witnesses

Revelation 11 is not in chronological order between the sixth and seventh trumpets. Some of the events we see do not even occur until the end of the Tribulation.

But chapter 11 does have to do with the general time frame surrounding the seventh trumpet, which occurs in verse 15. This is the midpoint of the Tribulation, and it is the first firm time reference we have to identify the return of the Lord. This reference resolves the mystery of the timing of the Lord's return.

At the midpoint of the Tribulation, the 144,000 Jewish evangelists will be raptured. That is in Revelation 12. It is also at that point that the Antichrist will be completely revealed for who he is. Then the last thing God will do at mid-Tribulation is raise up His two witnesses who will continue the proclamation of His Word throughout the last three-and-a-half years of the Tribulation.

The first part of chapter 11 gives us a look at these witnesses and their ministry.

> Then I was given a reed like a measuring rod. And the angel stood, saying, "Rise and measure the temple of God, the altar, and those who worship there. But leave out the court which is outside the temple, and do not measure it, for it has been given to the Gentiles. And they will tread the holy city underfoot for forty-two months."
>
> Revelation 11:1,2

How long is that? Three-and-a-half years. Here is another reference to what Daniel 9 and Matthew 24 called the **abomination of desolation,** the Antichrist's setting himself up to be worshipped instead of God and his attempts to destroy the children of God. That will continue for the last three-and-a-half years of the Tribulation.

The Two Witnesses

However, during this time, Jesus says He will give power to His two witnesses:

> "And I will give power to my two witnesses, and they will prophesy one thousand two hundred and sixty days, clothed in sackcloth."
>
> Revelation 11:3

By the Jewish calendar, that is also three-and-a-half years. All during the last half of the Tribulation, these two witnesses will proclaim the Word of God with great power.

> These are the two olive trees and the two lampstands standing before the God of the earth. And if anyone wants to harm them, fire proceeds from their mouth and devours their enemies. And if anyone wants to harm them, he must be killed in this manner.
>
> These have power to shut heaven, so that no rain falls in the days of their prophecy; and they have power over waters to turn them to blood, and to strike the earth with all plagues, as often as they desire.
>
> Revelation 11:4-6

The lampstand always represents God's purpose in a person or a nation. The olive trees, being the source of oil, represent the anointing—that power within us because we are a unique people and the Spirit of God indwells and inhabits each of us.

The two witnesses are going to have such an anointing to accomplish the purpose of God, even during the darkest hour of human history, that the Antichrist can raise no obstruction to successfully thwart their purpose of preaching the Word. They will have incredible power.

Murdered in the Streets

When they finish their testimony, the beast that ascends out of the bottomless pit will make war against them, overcome them, and kill them.

Revelation 11:7

When their course is finished and their testimony is done, the Antichrist will kill them.

And their dead bodies will lie in the street of the great city which spiritually is called Sodom and Egypt, where also our Lord was crucified.

Revelation 11:8

(The church has argued for centuries about who these two witnesses are. But it really does not matter.)

Then those from the peoples, tribes, tongues, and nations will see their dead bodies three-and-a-half days, and not allow their dead bodies to be put into graves. And those who dwell on the earth will rejoice over them, make merry, and send gifts to one another, because these two prophets tormented those who dwell on the earth.

Revelation 11:9,10

These two witnesses are going to give the Antichrist and those who have aligned their lives with him a rough time for three-and-a-half years.

The Antichrist will finally kill them, and He will think he has triumphed. But God will still be in total control.

The Antichrist is going to celebrate his victory on a worldwide scale to demonstrate his supreme power and authority. All over the world, people will be watching, partying and celebrating because they will feel free from the conviction they felt from the ministry of these two.

Alive Again

Now after the three-and-a-half days the breath of life from God entered them, and they stood on their feet, and great fear fell on those who saw them. And they heard a loud voice from heaven saying to them, "Come up here." And they ascended to heaven in a cloud, and their enemies saw them.

Revelation 11:11,12

What a powerful event! I am sure the similarities to the ministry of Jesus have not been lost on you. The ministry of Jesus lasted three-and-a-half years; the ministry of the two witnesses will last three-and-a-half years.

They will not be able to be touched by the enemy until their course is finished and they have accomplished what God will send them to do and they are ready, just as Jesus was.

They will be publicly displayed as dead for three days; Jesus was dead three days. They will be raised from the dead; Jesus was raised from the dead. Jesus ascended into heaven in a cloud; they will ascend to heaven in a cloud.

To me, this points out that the Lord intends their ministry to ultimately produce the same effect on a worldwide basis that Jesus' ministry, death and resurrection produced on a localized basis.

The resurrection and ascension of Jesus had a huge impact only on a localized basis because the people of His time on earth lacked the technical ability to broadcast the news very far beyond their immediate area. Of course, word of mouth and the preaching of the gospel took it to the whole world eventually.

Because this will be the final event before the return of Jesus, God will do everything He can to bring many into the body of Christ before Jesus returns. This will be it—the grand finale! When the two witnesses are raised and ascend to heaven, the last major event, an earthquake, will occur, and Jesus will return.

This is the third rapture. There have been three raptures in the book of Revelation: the Rapture of the church at the beginning of the Tribulation, the rapture of the 144,000 at the midpoint of the Tribulation, and the rapture of the two witnesses at the end of the Tribulation.

Interestingly enough, there were three raptures in the Old Testament as well: Enoch, who walked with God (as does the church), was raptured. Elijah, who spoke God's Word (as will the 144,000 Jewish evangelists), was raptured. And finally, Jesus, who demonstrated the kingdom of God with power (as will the two witnesses), was raptured.

Is this just a coincidence? I don't think so.

Why Two Witnesses?

In the same hour there was a great earthquake, and a tenth of the city fell. In the earthquake seven thousand men were killed, and the rest were afraid and gave glory to the God of heaven.

Revelation 11:13

The divine signature on the work of the two witnesses will be this earthquake as they ascend into heaven. This will be the earthquake which will come after the seventh vial and close out the events on the earth prior to the return of the Lord. It is mentioned again in chapter 17.

When I studied the two witnesses and looked at the similarities between their ministries and the ministry of Jesus, the question occurred to me, "Why are there two of them? If the Lord wanted to impact things as He did with the ministry of Jesus, why not just have one guy? What is the significance of there being two of them?"

Confirmation! God always confirms His Word in the mouth of two witnesses. (Jesus was the exception because He is the living Word Himself.) But the Word of God must be confirmed in the mouth of two witnesses. They will come to proclaim the Word. There must be two of them for the Word to impact people with the necessary power.

Second Corinthians 13:1 says, **"By the mouth of two or three witnesses every word shall be established."** Every word God speaks to your heart is going to be established or confirmed in the mouth of two or three witnesses. Every word.

Confirming the Word

We are indwelt by the Spirit of God, and He leads from within by impression, by generating desire, by inward knowings and by what the Bible calls **a still small voice.** (1 Kings 19:12).

But so often we know ourselves so well that we are reluctant to respond solely to the desires of our hearts and the things we feel impressed to do; we are just not sure if we really ought to trust ourselves.

This is why confirmations come by the mouth of two or three witnesses. God is not going to run twenty-five or thirty people by you; if you are not paying attention, you could miss the blessing of God. But when God is leading you to do something, He will always confirm it. Always. Somebody else will say something. And it will be a credible person whom you will be able to respond to and receive from.

God does not *direct* you by another's prophecy; He *confirms* what He has already spoken to your heart. Someone came up to me one time and told me he had a "major word from the Lord" for me. I appreciated his boldness and courage in bringing that word to me, but what he said was news to me.

I knew something was wrong, because God does not direct by prophecy. I never had any inkling or desire to do what this man said the Lord was telling him I should do. I wrote it off right there. God deals with us first, then confirms it through others.

But the other reason I was cautious was that I had never seen the guy before. God will always send someone whom He knows I can receive from, someone I can respond to; otherwise, it will not be a confirmation to me.

God said **two or three** witnesses, not "ten or twenty." Now, there have been times when He ran a dozen folks by me, but that was His mercy. As we are growing in the Lord, He will do that. But as a matter of course, it is two or three.

You must be reading the Word of God and listening carefully to the Spirit of God to know how He leads you and to be aware of these confirmations when they come. When you are feeling led of the Lord to do something, you'd better start waiting for these witnesses to come.

In His Timing

One other thing: Do not forget that timing is everything. By the Spirit, God may show you something He wants you to do—but not right now. I have seen many people jump out and do things on the strength of the desire in their hearts. But they missed God's timing.

Very often, the witnesses will be used to confirm not only the rightness of the Word you have received, but the timing for doing it as well.

One time, I really wanted to publish a magazine for my church; I knew the Lord had it in our ministry's future. But it was something I had seen in my spirit and desired so strongly that I felt it was supposed to be *right then*. So I went out and recruited an editor and a publisher and raised the money to do it. And it failed.

Remember, God does not live in the dimension of time, so any word from Him will always feel like *now*. The Lord made it clear to me from that experience that when the timing is right, resource availability will confirm it. When a couple of people came to me burning with the desire to do a magazine, I did not have to recruit anyone. They came looking for an opportunity to serve. God had directed them to do this and to volunteer their time for it. I knew then that the magazine was God's idea; these people were my confirmation. It was also an indicator of right timing.

This is how you walk by faith. You step out with your desires which have been confirmed in the mouth of two witnesses. It is one of your greatest safety nets against making errors.

Do not step out on the desire the Lord has placed in your heart until you are sure of the confirmations. But when two or more confirmations, or witnesses, have come, do not sit there and whine for another sign from God. Be aware that the confirmations are indicators of the timing of God's plan, or you could miss the boat altogether.

This process must become a regular part of your approach to decision making. God will honor your step of faith. He will show you something else and give you another desire, more confirmation, more steps. It is a wonderful adventure.

CHAPTER TWENTY-THREE

The Seventh Trumpet

The second woe is past. Behold, the third woe is coming quickly. Then the seventh angel sounded: And there were loud voices in heaven, saying, "The kingdoms of this world have become the kingdoms of our Lord and of His Christ, and He shall reign forever and ever!"

Revelation 11:14,15

The last and most significant event of the seventh trumpet is that Satan and his hosts will be cast out of heaven. (I want a front row seat for this event!)

And war broke out in heaven: Michael and his angels fought against the dragon; and the dragon and his angels fought, but they did not prevail, nor was a place found for them in heaven any longer. So the great dragon was cast out, that serpent of old, called the Devil and Satan, who

deceives the whole world; he was cast to the earth, and his angels were cast out with him.

Revelation 12:7-9

This seems like a flashback to the original angelic rebellion, when Lucifer was first cast out of heaven and became Satan. This is not the case. This is not a flashback; it is an event which will not occur until the seventh trumpet.

"Therefore rejoice, O heavens, and you who dwell in them! Woe to the inhabitants of the earth and the sea! For the devil has come down to you, having great wrath, because he knows that he has a short time."

Revelation 12:12

This is one of the *woe* judgments visited upon the inhabitants of the earth. Just remember, the first angelic rebellion is distinctly different from this one.

Back in Heaven

This raises a question. If Satan is cast out of heaven in Revelation 12, and that event is different from his initial rebellion when he was cast out of heaven, how did he get back into heaven?

This is particularly confusing if you believe—as many teachers suggest—that the devil operates out of hell. However, I do not believe that is scriptural.

We know Satan's demonic hosts, with the exception of the few angels who are chained in the bottomless pit until the Day of Judgment, operate in the earth. They are not consigned to hell—at least not yet.

You must understand how Satan regained access to heaven and to God after his expulsion. Man was created with authority over this earth, but he bowed his knee to Satan in the Garden of Eden. Satan usurped the authority intended for Adam, and that authority included access to God.

When Adam gave up his God-given dominion to Satan, the devil became the god of this world, legally entitled to manipulate unwitting people and circumstances to promote his purposes in the earth. By contrast, God can only work through our will as we choose to allow Him to do so.

Satan remains the god of this world until the end of this dispensation; the authority he has gives him access to the heavenly realm. We see this demonstrated in the book of Job.

Job's Example

Now there was a day when the sons of God came to present themselves before the Lord, and Satan also came among them.

Job 1:6

Sons of God is a term which usually refers to the angelic host—usually the higher orders of that host, such as archangels.

Scripture says there was a day designated when they presented themselves before the Lord. These angels have governing authority over this planet, so I suppose it was much like reporting to their commanding officer and receiving direction or instruction. That seems to be the picture here. Satan now has the authority over planet earth, and he has the same access to God as the rest of the angels.

We see it again in Job 2:1:

Again there was a day when the sons of God came to present themselves before the Lord, and Satan came also among them to present himself before the Lord.

I would imagine the rest of the angelic host came with the intent of carrying out the will of God and promoting His purpose in creation; however, Satan's purpose is to be the "the accuser of the brethren." (Rev. 12:10.)

Satan is the greatest legalist who ever lived. He knows and understands that God and His Word are one. He will come before the Judge of the universe—you can almost view this as a courtroom scene—and he will begin accusing the brethren.

He will say, "Look what she did. You have to judge her for this. Your law says…. You said in Your Word…so make the judgment, God." That is what he did with Job.

Here is the key to understanding the book of Job. The sole reason Job suffered what he did was that he did not have a mediator, or advocate, to represent his interests in the heavenly arena. We do! Jesus is described as our High Priest, our Mediator and our Advocate. He is all of that on our behalf because Satan is still in the heavenly arena as the accuser of the brethren and will be until the seventh trumpet.

Partaking of the Advocate Ministry of Jesus

Satan is *still* acting as the accuser of the brethren today. If you do not want to experience what Job did, you must learn how to lean upon your Mediator and Advocate.

Many people, primarily due to religious influence, read the book of Job and say, "This is an example of Christian suffering." Wrong. Job is an example of what we do *not* have to suffer, because we have a Mediator and an Advocate.

There are other contributing factors to Job's suffering. He had no covenant with God. He had no Word of God. He had no Spirit of God. He had nothing to tell him about God. He did not know the will of God. So he made statements out of ignorance, such as, **"The Lord gave, and the Lord has taken away; blessed be the name of the Lord"** (Job 1:21). People quote that verse thinking they are being spiritual. Job said that because he was ignorant of the will of God and the Word of God.

We do not have to suffer the judgments Satan would like to impose on our lives. We have a Mediator, an Advocate, a High Priest who is standing there every time an accusation is made against us. On our behalf, He says to the Father, "No, they are Mine. It is not their righteousness You are looking at, but the righteousness of God through Me, because I paid the price to free them from sin." Satan is not our judge; God is, and He is our Father.

Jesus, Our High Priest

Job knew what his problem was:

**"For He is not a man, as I am, that I may answer Him,
and that we should go to court together. Nor is there any
mediator between us, who may lay his hand on us both."**

Job 9:32,33

Job nailed the problem. He said, "I do not have anyone to stand between me, an unrighteous man, and a holy Creator, a holy God. I need a mediator." This is precisely what we have because of the availability of Jesus' high priestly ministry. That is what a high priest does—represents man before God. We may be a royal priesthood, but we still need a high priest to be our advocate before the Father. And our Advocate has never lost a case!

For this reason, you do not have to experience boils or sores or premature deaths in your family or any of what Job had to contend with. Financial calamity, relational problems, difficulties, crises or catastrophes—you do not have to experience those things.

Laying Hold of Jesus' Advocacy

Until the seventh trumpet sounds, which has not happened yet, Satan will still be in heaven accusing the brethren, which includes *you*. You need to lay hold of Jesus' high priestly advocate ministry for yourself. Just because Jesus is there does not mean He is yours.

How do you do that?

First, you must be born again. Jesus makes it clear that the only access to God is through Him. Jesus is not just our High Priest; He is our High Priest after the order of Melchizedek. (Heb. 6:20-7:3.)

Why Melchizedek? Melchizedek did two things: He received tithes from Abraham, and he conferred blessing. So second, you must pay your tithes. Your scriptural recognition of the high priestly ministry of Jesus is the payment of your tithe. I do not care if that bothers you; it is what the Word says. The folks who continue to dance around this issue just to save a few bucks are the ones who lose the most. The Word says that in order to receive blessings from God, you have to acknowledge His high priestly ministry by the payment of your tithes.

Third, you approach God in the name of Jesus. He said **"Whatever you ask in My name, that I will do"** (John 14:13).

Fourth, He is **the Apostle and High Priest of our confession** of faith (Heb. 3:1); So when you approach God, you do it through Jesus with a confession of faith. He is not the high priest of your profession of doubt and unbelief, of complaining and groaning.

So, in review, if we want to appropriate Jesus' high priestly ministry, we become born again, we become tithers, we approach God in the name of Jesus and we do it with confessions of faith.

Then we may expect to be delivered from the kinds of experiences Job had and to have a wonderful new experience of life. And someday soon the day will be here when, at the last trumpet, the accuser of the brethren will finally be given the boot!

CONCLUSION

Our study of Revelation has carried us to a major turning point in history. We've traveled to the very edge of the millennial reign of Christ. John has even given us a few peeks over into that glorious era.

In the process, we've discovered many important truths that are exceptionally relevant to our daily lives as we endeavor to live these exciting and momentous last days to the fullest. We have also had a sobering look at the days that will immediately follow the Rapture of the church.

Most importantly, we've learned how to make sure we see those awful days from the vantage point of heaven, rather than experiencing them here on earth.

There is obviously much more of the book of Revelation to explore. But for the purposes of this study, this is a good place to close. Perhaps in another volume, we will have the opportunity to dig into the second half of Revelation and mine the truths there.

I have tried to give you a fresh look at the days ahead and what they have in store for us, the world and the kingdom of God. We live in the most exciting time of all recorded history. We are the generation of the last millennium! We will see the fulfillment of all things—even those things the prophets longed for and did not see. We are the generation who will welcome our returning King!

ENDNOTES

Chapter 1
[1] Vine, s.v. "looking," Vol. 3, pp. 14,15.

Chapter 2
[1] Vine, s.v. "blessed," Vol. 1, pp. 132,133.

Chapter 3
[1] Strong, "Greek," entry #32, p. 7.
[2] Hagin, p. 15.

Chapter 4
[1] *The American Heritage Dictionary,* 2d College Ed., s.v. "delight."

Chapter 5
[1] Strong, "Greek," entry #2347, p. 36.
[2] Vine, s.v. "affliction," Vol. 1, pp. 37-39.
[3] Vine, s.v. "life," Vol. 2, pp. 336-338.
[4] Vine, s.v. "faithful," Vol. 2, p. 72.

Chapter 6
[1] *The American Heritage Dictionary,* 2d College Ed., s.v."mark."

Chapter 7
[1] *The American Heritage Dictionary,* 2d College Ed., s.v. "evangelize."
[2] Vine, s.v. "reasoned," Vol. 3, pp. 252,253.

Chapter 8
[1] *The American Heritage Dictionary,* 2d College Ed., "tradition."

Chapter 9
[1] *The American Heritage Dictionary,* 2d College Ed., s.v. "zeal."
[2] Vine, s.v. "look," Vol. 3, pp. 14,15.

Chapter 11
[1] Strong, "Greek," entry #1857, p. 30.
[2] Strong, "Greek," entry #4655, p. 65.
[3] *The American Heritage Dictionary,* 2d College Ed., s.v. "shame."

Chapter 13
[1] *The American Heritage Dictionary,* 2d College Ed., s.v. "profane."

Chapter 14
[1] Vine, s.v. "kingdom," Vol. 3, pp. 294-296.

Chapter 15
[1] Strong, "Hebrew," entry #2852, p. 45.
[2] Strong, "Hebrew," entry #7620, p. 111.
[3] Vine, s.v. "mystery," Vol. 3, pp. 97,98.

Chapter 16
[1] *The American Heritage Dictionary,* 2d College Ed., s.v. "falling away."

Chapter 17
[1] *The American Heritage Dictionary,* 2d College Ed., s.v. "judgment."

Chapter 18
[1] Acts 8:39; 2 Corinthians 12:2,4; 1 Thessalonians 4:17

Chapter 20
[1] Eerdman, s.v. "Abaddon"
[2] Strong, "Greek," entry #3338, p. 47.
[3] Strong, "Greek," entry #4991, p. 70.

Chapter 21
[1] Strong, "Greek," entry #32, p. 7.
[2] Deuternomy 8:3; Matthew 4:4; Jeremiah 15:16
[3] Vine, s.v. "mystery," Vol. 3, pp. 97,98

REFERENCES

The American Heritage Dictionary, 2d College Ed. Boston: Houghton Mifflin, 1992.

Eerdmans, William B. *The Eerdmans' Bible Dictionary.* Grand Rapids: William B. Eerdmans' Publishing Company, 1987.

Hagin, Kenneth E. *How You Can Be Led By The Spirit of God.* Tulsa: Kenneth Hagin Ministries, Inc., 1978.

Strong, James. *Strong's Exhaustive Concordance of the Bible.* Compact Edition. Grand Rapids: Baker Book House, 1985.

Vine, W. E. *Vine's Expository Dictionary of Old and New Testament Words.* Old Tappan: Fleming H. Revell Company, 1981

ABOUT THE AUTHOR

Mac Hammond is founder and senior pastor of Living Word Christian Center, a 5500+ member, nondenominational church in Minneapolis, Minnesota. He also hosts a weekly one-hour and half-hour television broadcast called *The Winner's Way With Mac Hammond,* seen nationwide; and a daily 60-second television commentary called *The Winner's Minute.*

Pastor Hammond has authored several internationally distributed books including *Angels at Your Service* and *Seeing and Knowing.*

Mac has been married to his wife Lynne for more than thirty years. Lynne is a nationally known speaker and author on the subject of prayer.

Mac Hammond, a former air force pilot and business leader, is broadly acclaimed for his ability to apply the Word of God to practical situations and the challenges of daily living.

To contact Mac Hammond,

write:

Mac Hammond Ministries

P. O. Box 29469

Minneapolis, MN 55429

Please include your prayer requests and comments when you write.

THE HARRISON HOUSE VISION

Proclaiming the truth and the power
Of the Gospel of Jesus Christ
With excellence;

Challenging Christians to
Live victoriously,
Grow spiritually,
Know God intimately.